Robotics and Medicine

Other titles in the *Next-Generation Medical Technology* series include:

Genetics and Medicine
Nanotechnology and Medicine
3D Printing and Medicine
Virtual Reality and Medicine

NEXT-GENERATION MEDICAL TECHNOLOGY

Robotics and Medicine

Kathryn Hulick

ReferencePoint Press®

San Diego, CA

© 2018 ReferencePoint Press, Inc.
Printed in the United States

For more information, contact:
ReferencePoint Press, Inc.
PO Box 27779
San Diego, CA 92198
www.ReferencePointPress.com

LIBRARY OF CONGRESS CATALOGING-IN-PUBLICATION DATA

Name: Hulick, Kathryn, author.
Title: Robotics and Medicine/by Kathryn Hulick.
Description: San Diego, CA: ReferencePoint Press, Inc., 2018. | Series:
  Next-Generation Medical Technology | Audience: Grade 9 to 12. | Includes
  bibliographical references and index.
Identifiers: LCCN 2017040830 (print) | LCCN 2017042233 (ebook) | ISBN
  9781682823309 (eBook) | ISBN 9781682823293 (hardback)
Subjects: LCSH: Robotics in medicine—Juvenile literature. | Medical
  technology—Juvenile literature. | Surgical robots—Juvenile literature.
Classification: LCC R857.R63 (ebook) | LCC R857.R63 H85 2018 (print) | DDC
  610.285—dc23
LC record available at https://lccn.loc.gov/2017040830

CONTENTS

1954
George Devol files a patent for the first industrial robot, which is eventually named Unimate.

1921
Karel Čapek coins the word *robot* for a science fiction play.

1950
Alan Turing imagines the Turing test for machine intelligence.

1960
Unimate goes to work on the General Motors automobile assembly line.

1977
R2-D2 and C-3PO first appear in the *Star Wars* trilogy.

1945   **1955**   **1965**   **1975**   **1985**

1968
HAL appears in the movie *2001: A Space Odyssey*.

1983
In the first use of robotics in the operating room, Arthrobot is used to hold and move patients' legs during surgery.

1942
Isaac Asimov's short story "Runaround" introduces the now-famous three laws of robotics.

1985
Surgeons use the PUMA 200 industrial robotic arm to perform part of a brain surgery.

1992
ROBODOC is introduced for hip replacement surgery.

2001
The first transatlantic surgery is performed using the ZEUS Robotic Surgical System.

1999
The da Vinci Surgical System debuts, ushering in the age of robotic surgery.

2001
Jesse Sullivan becomes the first person to control a robotic arm with his mind.

2011
IBM's Watson defeats human *Jeopardy!* champions.

1995   **2000**   **2005**   **2010**   **2015**

2000
Honda's ASIMO robot is the first real humanoid robot to walk on two legs.

2014
ReWalk is the first exoskeleton to receive FDA approval for use at home.

2016
STAR robot stitches together a pig intestine on its own, outperforming human surgeons.

Transforming Health Care

A robot lifts its head and gazes into an elderly patient's face. Lights rim the robot's eyes, changing color from blue to green as the machine gathers data. After a moment the robot knows that the patient's heart rate and breathing rate are normal. The patient asks the robot a few questions, nods at the replies, and then heads into the kitchen to make dinner. A few moments later the person falls with a thump. The robot cannot see or hear the impact, but it knows immediately that something is wrong. Its sensor that detects movement warns that the person is no longer moving. Another sensor knows that the stove is still on. So the robot calls for help. Soon a human nurse arrives, turns off the burner, and helps the patient get up.

This robot is called the IBM MERA, for Multi-Purpose Eldercare Robot Assistant. MERA is not ready to assist elderly people at home yet, but IBM is testing the robot at a lab at Rice University in Texas. The robot combines several cutting-edge technologies: a humanoid robot body called Pepper that can navigate the house, state-of-the-art sensors that monitor the environment and detect changes, and IBM's artificial intelligence (AI) software called Watson that can recognize and respond to human speech. This software is best known for defeating human champions on the quiz show *Jeopardy!* in 2011. But since that landmark victory, IBM has been applying Watson to new tasks, including health care.

The Doctor Shortage

Robots such as MERA are poised to transform the health care industry at a critical time. Several countries around the world are facing a similar dilemma. In the United States and Japan, the population of elderly people is growing faster than the working population. The Japanese Ministry of Health, Labor, and Welfare predicts that by 2025, the country will face a shortage of 1 million nurses and care workers. By that same year the United States will likely face a shortage of 500,000 nurses, according to *MD Magazine*. "Assistive, intelligent robots for older people could relieve pressures in hospitals and care homes as well as improving care delivery at home and promoting independent living for the elderly," says Irena Papadopoulos, founder of the European Transcultural Nursing Association.[1] Doctors are in short supply as well. Over the next decade the United States will likely need up to ninety thousand more doctors than are available, according to the Association of American Medical Colleges.

humanoid

resembling a human being

Japan, especially, is focusing on robotics as the answer to this problematic situation. The country is one of the world leaders in electronics and computing, and many innovations and breakthroughs in medical robotics have come from Japan. However, despite the progress being made on medical robots, these machines are not going to step in and take over every aspect of a nurse's or doctor's job, at least not any time soon. Rather, they are performing tasks that are boring, time consuming, or dangerous, or that require great accuracy and precision. They perform this work continuously without getting tired, becoming frustrated, or needing a vacation. The time and money that robots save frees up people to do more of the work that needs a human touch, such as talking a cancer patient through his or her options for treatment. "It is not a question of replacing human support but enhancing and complementing existing care," says Papadopoulos.[2]

Robots Among Us
Robots have already begun taking over low-skilled labor at hospitals and other medical facilities. Courier robots carry meals, medication, and fresh sheets to patient rooms, and cart trash and dirty

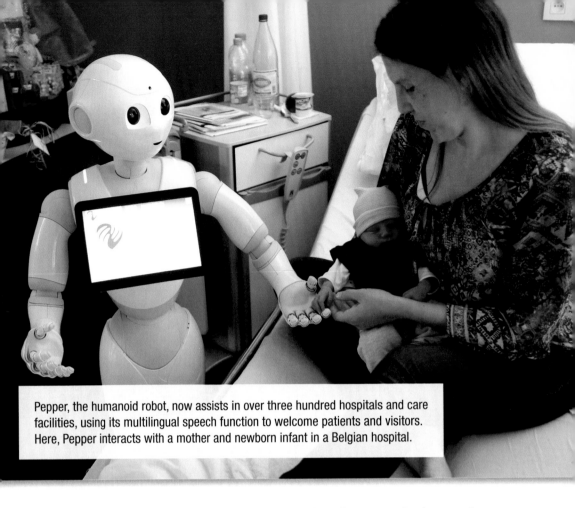

Pepper, the humanoid robot, now assists in over three hundred hospitals and care facilities, using its multilingual speech function to welcome patients and visitors. Here, Pepper interacts with a mother and newborn infant in a Belgian hospital.

laundry away. Cleaning robots disinfect floors and other surfaces. Pharmacy robots count and dispense medication. Robotic wheelchairs, exoskeletons, and bionic arms and legs help patients with limited mobility to get around and perform daily tasks. Some robots are doing jobs that are difficult and time consuming for even the smartest human, such as testing thousands of compounds during medical research or sorting through huge amounts of data to help doctors make a diagnosis.

Other robots are working directly with patients. Telepresence robots allow a doctor to interact with a patient from afar through a video conferencing screen and instrument attachments. Surgical robots are enhancing the accuracy and safety of surgery, augmenting a surgeon's vision with powerful cameras and replacing his or her hands with a suite of minuscule, precise instruments. Some of these robots are getting smart enough to perform repetitive aspects of surgery, such as suturing, on their own. Meanwhile, social robots such as MERA have learned to communicate with people in order to answer questions, provide basic physical or educational therapy, or entertain patients. "In the 21st century robots will increasingly be living among us," says Peter Dominey of CNRS, the French National Center for Scientific Research. "These robots must be able to take our perspective and co-operate with us and, if our plans change, they must be able to adjust their behavior accordingly. Most important of all, they must be safe."[3]

There is still a long way to go before a robot could take over the job of a human caretaker in the home, but robotics technology is improving every day. One day it may not be so strange for elderly people to remain in their homes

telepresence

the use of technology to remotely control a robot or mechanical system

much longer, thanks to the supervision and attention of a robot nurse like MERA. In the home and at school, robots might be able to diagnose and recommend treatment for minor health issues, while also offering an instant link to a human specialist through telepresence. In surgery, robots will get softer, smaller, and more flexible. They will enter the body without requiring an incision and perform operations with less and less human guidance. Some robots may shrink to minuscule dimensions, floating through the bloodstream to monitor health, make repairs, or destroy diseased cells. Robots will help us live longer, healthier lives.

CHAPTER 1

The First Robots

Before robots existed in real life, science fiction writers imagined remarkable machines that could match or even exceed human performance at a variety of tasks. The word *robot* was first used in a 1921 play by Karel Čapek. He and his brother invented the word based on a term from the Old Church Slavonic language, *robota*, meaning "forced labor." For several decades most science fiction stories portrayed robots as mindless metal villains. But then in the 1940s, writer Isaac Asimov popularized the idea of more humanlike robots that could act as heroes. Asimov even came up with three laws to govern robots' behavior. In his stories these laws were intended to ensure that robots were safe and obedient to their human masters. Since then, science fiction stories have imagined both good and bad roles for robots—from the lovable heroes C-3PO and R2-D2 in *Star Wars* to the spiderlike overlords that enslave humanity in *The Matrix*.

Real robots are not intelligent or competent enough yet to take on heroic or evil roles. But they are slowly, steadily pervading all aspects of human life. Today, to qualify as a robot, a machine must fit the following criteria: It must have moving parts, such as an arm or wheels; it must have one or more sensors to detect the outside world; and it must contain programming and controllers to help direct its actions. Some robots today add artificial intelligence to the mix. These robots can learn from experience or even make decisions on their own without human supervision. The medical industry is not the only one that relies on robots. Many other industries use the technology as well, including manufacturing, agriculture, education, defense, and more.

Even with artificial intelligence, today's robots remain much more like machines than the humanoid servants of science fiction. Real robots are designed to perform a specific task, such as vacuuming floors, dispensing medication, or delivering fresh sheets to hospital rooms. Developing a robot that could complete even these seemingly mundane tasks required years of research and technical advancement.

C-3PO and R2-D2 from the *Star Wars* franchise have helped popularize robots as friendly and helpful. Their capabilities to think, act independently, and even express fear have suggested to millions of fans that robots might someday become nearly human.

The Earliest Robots

It is impossible to name one single machine as the world's first robot. Tinkerers have been crafting robot-like machines, also called automatons, since ancient times. In the third century BCE, a Greek mathematician made a steam-powered mechanical bird. Automatons such as this delighted or amazed people, but they did not contain sensors or programming.

In the 1920s the Westinghouse Electric and Manufacturing Company produced a series of Televox robots. The first was named Herbert. Tasked with answering telephone calls, the "robot" was more like an answering machine made to look like a person with a crude, boxy shape. The same company also built Elektro the Moto-Man, a robot that could respond to a few voice commands with basic movements. Elektro amazed crowds at the 1939 and 1940 New York World's Fairs.

The Three Laws of Robotics

Isaac Asimov's three laws of robotics were introduced in 1942 in a fictional story titled "Runaround."

1. A robot may not injure a human being or, through inaction, allow a human being to come to harm.

2. A robot must obey the orders given it by human beings except where such orders would conflict with the First Law.

3. A robot must protect its own existence as long as such protection does not conflict with the First or Second Laws.

Asimov later added a "zeroth" law that states that a robot may not injure humanity or, through inaction, allow humanity to come to harm. These rules sound good, but they do not work so well in practice, as the plot in "Runaround" demonstrates. In the story two men send a robot named Speedy to gather materials to repair their space station. But Speedy runs into danger along the way. The robot knows that the men need the material to survive, but also knows that trying to get to the materials would likely result in its own destruction. The robot becomes stuck in a loop of indecision.

Isaac Asimov, *I, Robot.* New York: Doubleday. p. 40.

But robots did not enter the workforce until the 1950s. In the manufacturing industry, executives were looking for ways to speed up factory assembly lines. Machine tools performed some tasks faster or with more accuracy than humans. But these tools were each only designed to do one very specific task. Inventors started designing more complex machines that could be automated to perform a range of tasks. These industrial robots could speed up production and also take over tasks that were tedious or dangerous for humans. The Planet Corporation debuted its Planobot industrial robot in the mid-1950s, but the machine did not perform as well as promised, and only eight were sold.

Then, inventor George Devol and businessman Joseph Engelberger joined forces to create Unimate. They installed a prototype at a General Motors factory in 1959. It didn't look anything like a human. Its single metal arm extended from a massive base, and it weighed in at over 2,700 pounds (1,200 kg). But Unimate was a success, and Unimation became one of the first companies focused solely on robotics products. In 1966 Unimate appeared on television, delighting audiences with some tricks, including knocking a golf ball into a cup and pouring a drink. In 1969 General Motors rebuilt one of its plants to incorporate the robots and doubled the rate at which the factory produced cars. The single-armed structure of Unimate became standard for most industrial robots—in fact, these robotic arms quickly became an indispensable part of any factory floor. They could do many of the jobs that once belonged to human workers but with greater precision, speed, and strength.

As industrial robots took over factory floors, academics were experimenting with new robotics technology. In the late 1960s and early 1970s, researchers at the Stanford Research Institute (SRI) in California developed a robot named Shakey, now considered to be the first mobile robot with artificial intelligence. Shakey could detect its environment and make an internal model, like a map, of what it saw. It was the first robot that could get from one place to another without a human driver. "The ground rule was to keep it as mechanically simple as possible. That's why we don't have arms. . . . It looks like a washing machine on wheels," says Peter Hart, who worked on Shakey and later founded the electronics company Ricoh.[4] The method Shakey used to navigate has been adapted to many other mobile robots, including ones now used in health care.

From Factories to Brain Surgery

Students and researchers at Stanford University also made progress on robotic arms. In 1969 Victor Scheinman designed a new robotic arm that was one of the first to be controlled via a computer. It was smaller and more versatile than Unimate. Scheinman later sold the design to Unimation, which released an improved version in 1978 named the Programmable Universal Machine for Assembly, or PUMA.

Like its predecessors, PUMA was intended for factory use, but Yik San Kwoh and a group of doctors at Long Beach Memorial Medical Center in California had other ideas. They thought the robot's ability to drill a hole with excellent precision could make a difference in brain surgery. In 1985 Kwoh and his colleagues completed three brain surgeries with the help of a PUMA 200

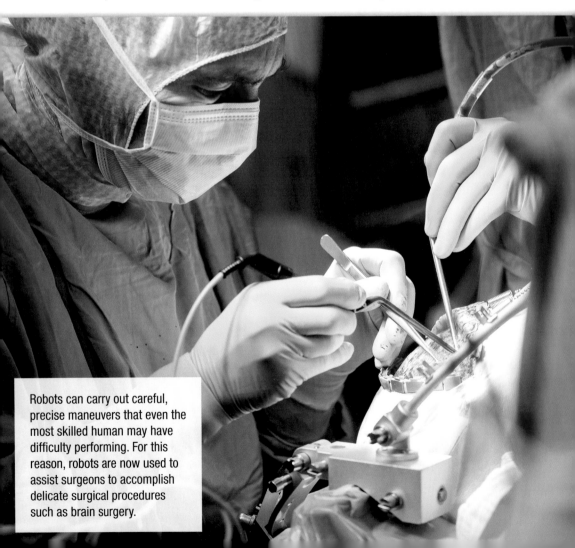

Robots can carry out careful, precise maneuvers that even the most skilled human may have difficulty performing. For this reason, robots are now used to assist surgeons to accomplish delicate surgical procedures such as brain surgery.

robotic arm. This was the very first use of a robot to perform surgery. The doctors practiced on watermelons first. Then they used a computer system to map the location of a tumor in a patient's brain. Finally, they fed the robot the exact location of the tumor, and had it drill a tiny hole through the brain to the target. When a human surgeon performs the procedure, a tiny tremor in the hand could cause permanent brain damage. "The robotic arm is safer, faster and far less invasive than current surgical procedures," Kwoh asserts.[5]

Surgical robots did not have to make incisions to be helpful during a procedure. Two years earlier, in 1983, Arthrobot had become the first robot used in an operating room. James McEwen and a team of biomedical engineers at Vancouver General Hospital in Canada developed Arthrobot in order to hold a patient's leg during surgery on the knee. The human surgeon used voice commands to direct the robot to reposition the leg. "Holding a limb in place for long periods of time can be very fatiguing [for humans]," states McEwen. "The robot doesn't get tired and it doesn't get bored."[6]

From the mid-1980s through the 1990s, other early surgical robots were developed, each for a specific type of procedure. In hip replacement surgery, for instance, ROBODOC helped prepare the hip joint to ensure that an implanted hip would fit perfectly. In prostate surgery, PROBOT helped remove soft tissue. The procedure requires many repeated cuts to reduce the size of the prostate, a gland that can swell as men age, making it difficult to urinate. Robotics technology offered many benefits to surgeons, including consistent stability, pinpoint accuracy, and an increased range of motion.

> **laparoscopy**
>
> surgery performed by inserting a camera and surgical instruments through a tiny incision

Operating from a Distance

During the late 1980s a new form of surgery was rising in popularity. Laparoscopy was a surgical technique that involved making one or two tiny incisions, then inserting a camera called an endoscope to see inside the body. The surgeon would also place long surgical instruments through the tiny incisions, then manipulate them like knitting needles while watching the feed from the camera on a video screen. The smaller size of the incisions made surgery safer. Patients also recovered more quickly. However, manipulating laparoscopic instruments was really difficult. "Surgeons had to give up their 3D vision. They had to give up their wrists. They had to give up intuitive motion in the instruments," says Catherine Mohr, vice president of Intuitive Surgical, a company that makes surgical robots.[7]

Robotic systems were soon developed to assist with laparoscopic procedures. The Automated Endoscopic System for Optical Positioning (AESOP) 3000 would hold and move the camera during a laparoscopic procedure. The next-generation version of this robot, the ZEUS Robotic Surgical System, had three robotic arms that the surgeon directed. One arm held the camera while the other two could make incisions and extractions. Using a robotic system like this, the surgeon could perform his or her work from a comfortable seated position, and could manipulate the instruments in a much more intuitive manner than traditional laparoscopy.

endoscope

a medical instrument with a camera at the tip that is inserted into the body to view internal areas

Technically, the surgeon did not even have to be in the same room as the patient. As long as the surgeon's console could transmit and receive data from the robot quickly and smoothly enough, then they could be in different rooms, different cities, or even different countries. An important milestone for telepresence surgery came in 2001, when surgeons located in New York used the ZEUS system to remove the gallbladder from an elderly female patient in Strasbourg, France.

Robo Arms and Legs
Robotics technology has also made a difference in the medical field of rehabilitation. Assistive medical devices such as prosthetic arms and legs, crutches, and wheelchairs have been around for centuries. However, robotics technology has improved these

devices and added new ones, allowing people with disabilities or missing limbs greater freedom and control over their lives. In the early 1960s, the Case Institute of Technology developed a robotic arm intended to assist people who were unable to use their own arms. The arm had four degrees

of freedom. In robotics each degree of freedom adds to the range of movement. For example, a robotic wrist with three degrees of freedom might move up and down, or left and right, or around in a circle. Also during the 1960s, the Rancho Los Amigos rehabilitation hospital in California developed a robotic arm with seven degrees of freedom. This allowed the device to move more like a real human arm. Some of these early manipulator arms were mounted to wheelchairs.

By the 1980s assistive devices had become more complex. Johns Hopkins University developed a workstation intended to

Job Thieves

As robots have become more and more capable, they have taken over roles that once belonged to human workers. Factories no longer have to employ as many human laborers as they once did thanks to robots. Low-skilled workers are most at risk of losing a job to new technology. In health care, robots have already begun to perform work that typically belongs to janitors and hospital orderlies, including cleaning and disinfecting surfaces, delivering food and supplies to hospital rooms, and assisting patients with basic tasks such as getting out of bed. Robots are also beginning to dispense medication, so they could replace some pharmacy positions. But others believe that robots are good news for these workers. "In healthcare we're trying to move people away from doing things that are menial, that could be done by machines, and training them to do higher level services," says Mark Laret of the University of California–San Francisco Medical Center. "People are concerned about loss of jobs, but the bigger issue I think is we can deploy people to doing things they're better suited to doing than machines, and have the machines do the menial work. That's how we want to grow." Some people may lose their jobs, but new technology also opens up new and better jobs for human beings.

Quoted in Andrew Zaleski, "Behind Pharmacy Counter, Pill-Packing Robots Are on the Rise," CNBC, November 15, 2016. Video. www.cnbc.com.

assist a person with little to no ability to move on his or her own, such as a person paralyzed from the neck down. The workstation allowed a user to eat, read, or use a computer by manipulating the robotic system with chin motions. Robotics technology has helped make prosthetic legs more lifelike as well.

Humanoids

None of these early medical robots looked humanoid because that shape did not fit their purpose. Surgical robots looked more like strange metal sea creatures sprouting multiple arms, while robotic prostheses resembled metal arms or legs. The function of the robot dictated its form. However, some robot functions require a more humanlike form. Humanoid robots could manipulate human tools in dangerous situations, such as a disaster response scenario or an outer space mission. In the medical industry, hu-

DRC-HUBO, a robot built by a South Korean team of engineers, completes a precision cutting task during the finals of the 2015 DARPA Robotic Challenge. Such contests help fuel interest in robotics and speed advances in the technology and capabilities of robots.

manoid robots could help care for sick or elderly patients. People are more likely to trust a robot with a face and body that roughly resemble a human's.

In 2000 the Japanese automotive company Honda started producing a humanoid robot named ASIMO that could walk on two legs and perform basic tasks, such as turning on lights or opening and closing doors. The idea was that the robot could assist people who could not easily do these things on their own. However, ASIMO is not yet ready to take on this role in an elderly or disabled person's home. It mainly interacts with the public at trade shows and conventions. Honda continues to work on new versions of the robot with the goal of bringing it into people's homes. "ASIMO is a robot that captures the imagination, intrigues the intellect and stimulates people to dream of the future by seeing the possibilities of today," said Jeffrey A. Smith of Honda when ASIMO was inducted into the Robot Hall of Fame in 2004.[8]

Building a robot that can navigate unpredictable environments and perform a variety of tasks has proved to be a huge engineering challenge. In 2015 DARPA, the Defense Advanced Research Projects Agency, an arm of the US Department of Defense, sponsored a contest for robots featuring an obstacle course with tasks such as driving a vehicle, crossing over a pile of rubble, climbing a ladder, and using a power tool. The $2 million prize went to DRC-HUBO, a robot crafted by Team KAIST from South Korea. Although the idea behind the contest was to promote the development of robots that could assist in a disaster, technological advances inspired by the contest will help improve robotics technology in all other industries as well, including medicine. Robots have come a long way from being assembly line machines that perform repetitive tasks. The more tasks robots are able to perform, the more people will come to depend on them.

CHAPTER 2

Robotic Surgery

In a hospital operating room, a da Vinci surgical robot hovers over an unconscious patient. The patient is here to have her appendix removed. This tiny organ hangs off the large intestine and serves no useful purpose. If it becomes diseased, surgeons must remove it to save the person's life. For the procedure, the patient and robot are both covered in protective draping. Beneath the sheets, the robots' arms sink into the patient's belly through tiny incisions. A camera in one of the arms transmits a high-resolution, three-dimensional view of the diseased appendix.

Other arms bear tiny pincers, cutters, or graspers. At a nearby console, a surgeon readies his feet over a pair of pedals and slides his fingers into a controller. As he twists his wrists and pinches his fingers, two tiny pincers at the surgery site mimic his motions, gently lifting up the appendix. He next uses the console to direct a grasping instrument to insert surgical thread and manipulates the pincers to sew a knot near where the appendix attaches to the large intestine. Then the surgeon uses the pincers to cut the appendix off, and removes it with the grasping tool. The robotic surgery is complete.

Superhuman Eyes and Hands

The da Vinci robot came out in 1999 and received approval from the Food and Drug Administration (FDA) in 2000. Its debut ushered in the age of robotic surgery. The da Vinci and similar systems vastly improved surgeons' vision, dexterity, steadiness, and comfort during laparoscopic procedures of all kinds. Surgeons now use these robots for everything from surgeries on the abdomen, intestines, and reproductive systems to heart or lung surgery. The da Vinci system alone has been used to perform over three million operations, according to the robot's producer, Intuitive Surgical. Many users believe that robotic surgery is better for both patients and their doctors. "From Day 1, when I sat down at that robotic console, I knew we would give patients a better outcome," says Dr. Vipul Patel. "I have not seen anyone who has done a good amount of robotic surgery go back."[9]

Surgeons such as Patel no longer have to rely only on their own eyes and hands to perform an operation. The robot's camera "eye" sees at resolutions and magnifications beyond human ability. The latest da Vinci system offers tenfold magnification, providing a view like nothing surgeons had experienced before. The ability of the camera to snake into small spaces also allows surgeons to see places in the body that had once been invisible during an operation. For example, surgeons used to have to operate on the inside of the pelvis by feel, since putting a human hand into the small space blocks the view. Surgical robots also supply extra arms and "hands" that offer a greater range of motion and more dexterity than human wrists and fingers. A surgeon can use one robotic arm to hold tissue in place, then two more to sew up an incision, while a third holds the camera. The system filters out any tremors or shaking, allowing the surgeon to perform delicate operations without any unwanted movement.

The main drawback of a system such as da Vinci is cost. These robots are large, complex pieces of machinery—as a result, they are extremely expensive. A hospital must spend between $1.5 million and $2 million to purchase and install a single da Vinci Surgical System. On top of that cost, the hospital must pay for regular service and for single-use tools that attach to the robotic arms. Each robotic surgery costs $1,000 to $2,000 more than a standard surgery, according to *Modern Healthcare* magazine. Small or rural hospitals may not be able to afford to buy or maintain the equipment. In addition it's not clear whether the high-tech procedure is actually safer than regular laparoscopic surgery or makes recovery any easier for patients. However, since the systems are high-tech and state of the art, most patients and doctors prefer them.

The da Vinci Surgical System has been the leading choice for robotic surgery since its introduction, but several companies are developing competing technology. Medtronic's new robotic system will likely be less expensive and able to perform more procedures

haptic

related to the sense of touch

than da Vinci. The company TransEnterix is developing a laparoscopic robotic surgery system called ALF-X. Unlike da Vinci, ALF-X tracks the surgeon's eyes and automatically moves the camera at the surgery site to follow his or her gaze. The system also offers haptic feedback, meaning that the surgeon can feel sensations through the controller as the tools touch tissues within the body. Both of these attributes could make the process of robotic surgery feel even more natural for the surgeon.

Intuitive Surgical, maker of the da Vinci, has made many improvements to its system as well. Firefly Fluorescence Imaging technology works in conjunction with the da Vinci system to help

fluorescence

light emitted by certain substances

surgeons better visualize the area of the body that requires surgery. To use the system, doctors inject a special dye into the patient's body. This dye glows bright green when viewed through a special camera. In kidney surgery to remove a tumor, for example, the surgeon can inject the dye so that it only flows through the healthy part of the organ. The tumor will appear dark. The dye could also be carried into the body by molecules designed to seek out cancer cells and bind to them. Then the cancer cells would glow, distinguishing them from healthy cells.

From Bone Cutters to Cancer Zappers

Da Vinci and its competitors can perform a wide range of surgical procedures, but some surgeries require very different tools and techniques. Robotics technology now assists with bone cutting, hip and knee replacements, hair transplants, cataract correction, cancer treatment, and more. The Cold Ablation Robot-guided Laser Osteotome, or CARLO for short, is a robotic system designed to cut through the skull or other bone using a high-tech laser beam. Conventional bone surgery uses a saw, which causes more damage to the body than the thin laser beam. In addition the robotic system can plan cuts on its own based on data from

Robotic Cardiac Surgery

Cardiac surgery with the da Vinci and similar robotic systems is less invasive than traditional surgery. It allows a surgeon to make smaller and more precise cuts, which means less chance of complications. Robotic surgery has been used for heart-related procedures such as coronary artery bypass, heart defect repair, and tumor removal. In this type of operation, the surgeon manipulates the robotic hands from a console while looking at a camera view of the heart.

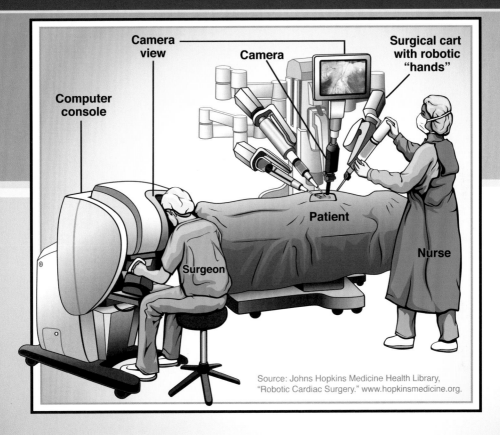

Source: Johns Hopkins Medicine Health Library, "Robotic Cardiac Surgery." www.hopkinsmedicine.org.

its sensors. "CARLO goes much further than the well-known da Vinci operations robot, which actually only does what the surgeons tell it," says Philippe C. Cattin of the University of Basel in Switzerland, who helped develop the robot.[10]

One of the first medical robots, ROBODOC, assisted with hip replacement surgery in 1992. Since then robots have remained an important part of hip and knee replacement surgeries. NAVIO, MAKO, and TSolution One are all state-of-the-art robots designed

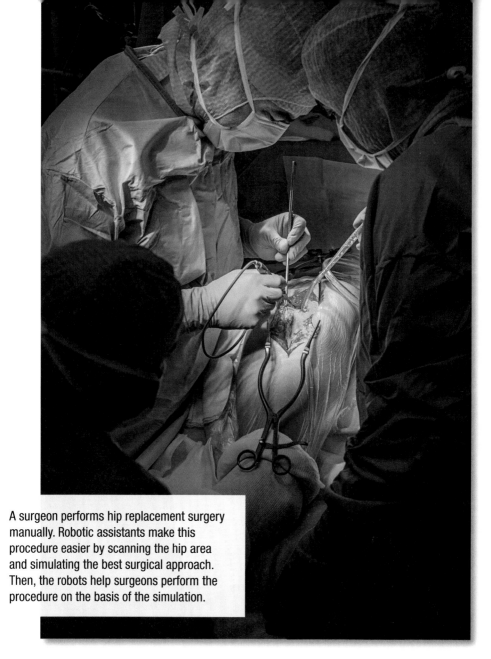

A surgeon performs hip replacement surgery manually. Robotic assistants make this procedure easier by scanning the hip area and simulating the best surgical approach. Then, the robots help surgeons perform the procedure on the basis of the simulation.

for these procedures. All of these systems first scan the patient's joint to produce a virtual 3-D model of that person's bones. The surgeon then prepares the operation on the basis of that model. During the actual procedure, the surgeon guides the robot through the plan to remove the problematic joint and make room for the implant. NAVIO can sense if the surgeon deviates from the plan. If this happens, the robot shuts off. If the deviation was intentional, the surgeon can override the shutdown.

ARTAS is a robot with a peculiar specialty. It harvests hair from one part of the head, then assists with the process of implanting that hair elsewhere. The procedure allows partially bald people to grow a full head of their own hair. Similar procedures that don't use a robot typically remove a large strip of hair, leaving a telltale mark. ARTAS has a better approach. It uses artificial intelligence to identify and select only the best hairs to harvest. One at a time, thousands of times, the robot selects a hair then punches it out of the scalp. Later the machine will help select locations for a doctor to implant the hairs.

Robots also assist with cancer treatments. Whenever possible, a surgeon will operate to remove a cancerous tumor, often using da Vinci or a similar system. However, sometimes the tumor is in a location that is too difficult or dangerous to reach with surgery, such as the brain, lungs, or spine. Or perhaps the cancer has begun to spread throughout the body. In these cases doctors will typically turn to radiation therapy. Radiation is high-energy light that kills cancer cells, yet it also kills healthy cells. So the more precisely a doctor can target the tumor, the better. CyberKnife is a robotic system that allows doctors to carefully zap tricky tumors. Scientists at Stanford started developing the first CyberKnife in the 1990s. Today's system employs a robotic arm that directs a very thin beam of radiation at the body from any angle. It can avoid hitting and damaging sensitive structures, such as the spinal cord or the eyes. It can also account for body motions, such as breathing. "When you're breathing, a lung tumor will move up and down," says Brian Thorndyke of Colorado CyberKnife, a facility that offers treatment with the robotic system.[11] He explains that CyberKnife can use its imaging system to track both the tumor and a marker placed on the patient's chest. As the marker moves up and down with each breath, the robot adjusts automatically.

Getting Smarter

CyberKnife, ARTAS, and many other medical robotic systems in use today are able to perform small segments of a procedure independently. CyberKnife tracks breathing on its own, and ARTAS selects hair follicles by itself. LASIK vision correction, a surgical procedure that uses lasers to reshape a person's eyes and restore clear vision, often uses robotic systems to plan the procedure and correct for eye movement during the operation. Some might argue that the da Vinci system is not actually a robot because it doesn't have the ability to move or make plans on its own—that is, a human surgeon must manipulate the tools. "We are at the infancy of the automation spectrum for medical robotics," says Corey Ryan of the medical robotics company KUKA Robotics Corporation in Michigan. "The [da Vinci] system doesn't do the work itself. It's simply a remote tool the doctor can use."[12] It's like a car that needs a human driver to go anywhere. But just as automotive engineers are developing self-parking, self-braking, and even self-driving cars, medical engineers are crafting surgical robots with similar abilities.

suture

to stitch together a wound or incision

Robotics engineers, or roboticists, at the University of California, Berkeley, are using an artificial intelligence technique called machine learning to train a da Vinci system to perform some procedures independently. To teach the robot how to suture, or stitch tissue together, the researchers had eight surgeons use the robot to make a series of stitches in pink rubber. Meanwhile, the robot recorded what was happening and divided up the task into segments, such as pushing the needle in and pulling it out. Then the robot tried to make some stitches on its own. The task isn't as easy as it may sound—the robot only succeeded half of the time. On many trials, it missed grabbing the needle or tangled the thread. But Ken Goldberg, who leads the research, is optimistic that autonomous robots will soon make a surgeon's job easier. "Our goal is to help surgeons focus on the critical aspects of surgery, rather than having to perform each tedious and repetitive subtask," he says.[13]

autonomous

able to operate independently

Machine learning opens up a world of possibilities for autonomous robots. When a robot can learn from experience and modify its own procedures on the basis of that data, then all it needs is access to training data in order to improve. Verb Surgical, a joint venture between Johnson & Johnson and Google, is working on a digital surgery platform that would help collect and analyze data from surgeries. If surgeons today were to record and share data on the thousands of operations they perform with surgical robots, then an autonomous version of the robot could use that data to learn how to suture or perform other tasks. "The system could extract the data, improve its algorithms, fine-tune the task," Goldberg says. "We'd be collectively getting smarter."[14]

In 2016 a surgical robot named STAR, for Smart Tissue Autonomous Robot, performed a real suturing operation entirely on its own. Human surgeons supervised but did not manually guide its instruments. The surgery involved stitching together a pig's small intestine in a procedure similar to repairing a break in a garden hose. To prove its ability, the robot performed this

Teleoperation

Since the da Vinci Surgical System was first introduced, researchers have pointed out numerous exciting applications for a system that allows a surgeon to operate from afar. In 2001 Dr. Michael Gagner of Miami's Mt. Sinai Medical Center, said, "As the technology evolves and becomes available . . . it will be useful for telementoring, teaching, and performing rare surgery that requires different expertise. A smaller city could have the help of an expert surgeon just by being connected."

Unfortunately, robots such as da Vinci still require the pristine environment of a hospital operating room. They are too large and too expensive to assist patients at disaster sites and battlefields or to be deployed in developing countries and rural areas. In 2005 DARPA launched the Trauma Pod program to develop a mobile operating room that could be dispatched in a war zone or natural disaster. A year later, researchers Jacob Rosen and Blake Hannaford of the University of Washington tested a prototype robot outdoors in a sandy, windy, hot area of southwestern California. A surgeon located at a control console about three hundred feet away operated on fake organs made of latex. The robot's power supply came from gasoline-fueled generators. "To develop a surgical robot that can operate in harsh environments, our group has focused on miniaturization and mobility," Rosen and Hannaford report. As surgical robots become smaller, more rugged, and cheaper, more and more people will gain access to lifesaving medical treatments.

Quoted in D.L. Parsell, "Surgeons in U.S. Perform Operation in France via Robot," National Geographic News, September 19, 2001. www.nationalgeographic.com.

Jacob Rosen and Blake Hannaford, "Doc at a Distance," IEEE Spectrum, September 29, 2006. http://spectrum.ieee.org.

procedure multiple times, both on intestines removed from a pig's body and on living pigs. When the researchers compared the stitches the robot made to ones made by human surgeons, the robot's were superior. "Even though we surgeons take pride in our craft at doing procedures, to have a machine that works with us to improve outcomes and safety would be a tremendous benefit," says lead researcher Peter Kim of Children's National Health System in Washington, DC.[15] Kim and his team imagine that surgeons may one day perform hands-free robotic surgery. In this scenario a surgeon would still give the robot commands, but would not manually manipulate its instruments.

Seeing into the Future

While some surgical robots are getting smarter and more autonomous, others are getting smaller, softer, and more flexible. The Dutch company Preceyes has developed a new robotic surgical system to perform eye surgery, called Robotic Retinal Dissection Device, or R2D2 for short. Inside the eye, precision matters. Even a tiny slip could result in damage to the eye. The new robotic system filters out any unsteadiness in the surgeon's hands and allows control over movements as slight as the width of a human hair. "My movements were improved and finessed by the robot," says Robert MacLaren of Oxford University in England.[16] Using R2D2, he performed the first ever robotic eye surgery in the fall of 2016. Before this milestone procedure, certain eye surgeries were impossible to perform. For example, age-related macular degeneration is a common but currently incurable eye disease that causes elderly people to lose their vision. Using a system such as R2D2, a doctor could hypothetically inject a drug to treat macular degeneration into a single vein within the eye. The veins there are thinner than human hairs. Such precision is impossible for the human hand but doable with a robot. This type of targeted drug therapy could also potentially cure some forms of blindness.

Soft, flexible machines are on the cutting edge of medical robotics research as well. Today's surgical robots are strong and durable likely because they developed from manufacturing robots, which had to put together cars and other products. It made sense to construct them from metal. But most surgeons operate on squishy, sensitive areas of the human body, where sharp metal

Age-related macular degeneration is a deterioration of a retinal pigment, causing a loss of vision in the center of the eye (simulated in this image). Robots can deliver drug therapies so precisely now that they might soon be able to help treat this deterioration by injecting medicine into the tiny veins of the eye.

parts may cause damage. In addition the interior of the human body twists and turns in contorted shapes. Metal, jointed robot limbs can only move on straight paths; therefore, some researchers are rethinking the basics of surgical robots. Rather than stiff metal machines, they have crafted twisting, soft robots that resemble snakes or the tentacles of an octopus. Or, in the case of the "heart hugger," the robot is a rubbery cap that fits over a human heart to help it beat. "If you look in biology . . . there are all kinds of incredible solutions to movement, sensing, gripping, feeding, hunting, swimming, walking and gliding that have not been open to hard robots," says chemist George Whitesides of Harvard University in Massachusetts. "The idea of building fundamentally new classes of machines is just very interesting."[17] Whitesides cofounded the Massachusetts company Soft Robotics to produce rubbery robotic grippers for use in industrial, food processing, and medical applications.

Medrobotics' Flex Robotic System resembles a snake that slides down a patient's throat or through another natural body opening. This allows the surgeon to operate in certain areas of the body without making any incisions. Flex was approved by the FDA in 2015. Dr. Umamaheswar Duvvuri used Flex to remove a growth from the back of a patient's tongue. Without this technology, Duvvuri would have had to cut through the patient's neck in order to reach the growth. Instead, he used a joystick to steer a metal tube down the patient's throat as a camera and light at the tip of the tube showed the way. When he reached the correct site, the tube stiffened to make a platform for the instruments, which snaked down through the main tube. Duvvuri performed the rest of the procedure via a control console, just as with a da Vinci system. "The concept of flexible robotics is going to be the next revolution in surgical advancements," predicts Duvvuri.[18]

If the experts are correct, a surgical robot of the future may look more like a squirming octopus than a metal claw. And that robot may have the ability to perform some parts of a surgery on autopilot, or with minimal direction from human surgeons. These surgical robots will likely make it easier and safer to perform operations that are difficult, dangerous, or even impossible today.

CHAPTER 3

Helper Bots

Robots that can remove an appendix, cut through bone, or zap tumors are some of the flashiest, most exciting examples of medical technology. But other, more mundane robots play a very important role in hospitals and the medical industry in general. These helper robots do jobs that would normally belong to hospital orderlies, nurses, janitors, and other human assistants. Hospitals have to manage the distribution of food, laundry, trash, and other supplies around the clock. Often these items must travel long distances. For example, a meal may need to get from the cafeteria on the ground floor to a patient's room on the top floor. In the past, people had to push heavy carts of supplies around to make all these deliveries. But robots have started to take over courier tasks in many hospitals. They also clean and disinfect surfaces and help dispense medication in pharmacies.

courier

a messenger

Making Deliveries

In 1988 a new hospital opened in San Diego. The Naval Medical Center featured a fleet of twenty-five robots, also known as automated guided vehicles (AGVs). They looked sort of like miniature refrigerators on wheels that traveled through the hospital in staff-only hallways and elevators, following wire tracks built into the floors. In a computer control room, a map tracked all of the robots. When summoned, for example, a robot would travel to a pickup station where it would use its forklift to load trays of food or other supplies. Then it carried the supplies to their destination. The robot would also carry trash and dirty laundry out of patient rooms. While some hospitals today still use AGV systems, robotics technology has advanced to the point where hidden tracks are no longer needed to guide robots.

Mobile robots that make deliveries got their start in manufacturing and distribution, where they help fetch and place items in huge warehouses. Toward the end of the first decade of the 2000s, though, companies began building courier robots intended to run errands in hospitals. Examples include Tug, QC Bot, Hospi, RoboCourier, and Terapio. Each is smart enough to find its own way around using computer vision, sensors, and internal maps. Tug rolls around approximately as fast as a walking person, emitting quiet "beeps" to let people know it's coming. If something or someone gets in its way, Tug stops, then navigates around the obstacle. It can talk, too, with preprogrammed phrases including, "Waiting for a clear elevator." At the University of California, San Francisco (UCSF) Medical Center at Mission Bay, Tug robots tote as much as 1,000 pounds (454 kg) of laundry and deliver one thousand meals every day. They can also deliver medication. Tug robots that carry drugs have a special access system so the drugs won't fall into the wrong hands. The doctor or nurse who ordered the drugs must unlock the robot using a fingerprint reader.

Courier robots such as Tug help a hospital run more efficiently. They allow human workers to spend more time on patient care or technical tasks, rather than running around making tedious and time-consuming deliveries. "By being more efficient we're able to devote more of our dollars toward paid employees at the bedside caring for patients," says Ken King of El Camino Hospital in California, which has been using Tug robots since 2009. Plus, most people seem to enjoy interacting with the robots. They move things out of the robots' way if they get stuck, and come up with cute nicknames for them. "We've named ours after fruit," says Dan Henroid, director of nutrition and food services at UCSF at Mission Bay. "So we have Apple, Grape, Banana, Orange, Pear—and Banana is out right now. At some point we'll get them skins so they actually look like the fruit."[19]

Hospi, a mobile delivery robot deployed at hospitals in Japan and Singapore, comes in several playful colors and its "head" features a computer screen with a smiling face. A hospital employee must use an ID card to unlock its contents. Autonomous mobile robots are also assisting in health care laboratories, where

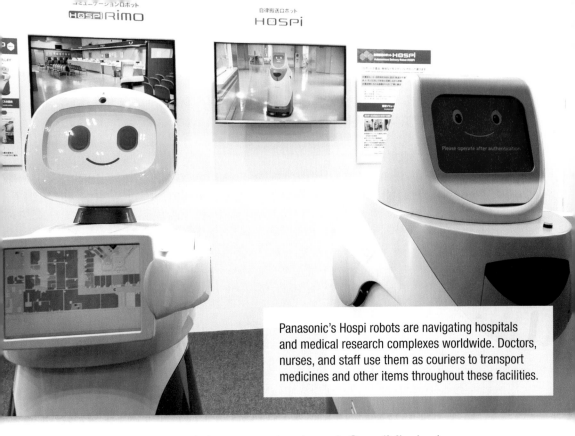

Panasonic's Hospi robots are navigating hospitals and medical research complexes worldwide. Doctors, nurses, and staff use them as couriers to transport medicines and other items throughout these facilities.

new treatments and drugs are developed. SpeciMinder is an autonomous mobile robot designed to carry medical specimens, research animals, and other materials around a laboratory. One SpeciMinder, nicknamed "Frances," works in a pathology lab at Christiana Care Health Systems in Delaware. That one robot has traveled over 25,000 miles (40,000 km) and made more than one hundred thousand deliveries, according to its manufacturer, CCS Robotics. These courier robots are all doing what a human would consider grunt work—just carrying things from place to place. But the robots employ highly sophisticated technology to safely navigate a busy environment and complete their errands.

Keeping Things Squeaky Clean

Robots are also starting to take over some hospital cleaning duties. When sick people come to the hospital, they may bring germs and viruses with them. Those germs could stick around and sicken others. People who are going through surgery or other treatments are especially susceptible to acquiring an infection while in the hospital. This is so common that there's even a special name for it—a health care–associated infection. To try to avoid these infections, hospitals devote a lot of time and effort to keeping surfaces, floors, and equipment squeaky clean. But robots promise to make hospital-cleaning tasks quicker, easier, and more thorough.

Many people are already familiar with cleaning robots and may even have one at home. Roomba, a robotic vacuum cleaner, and Scooba, a robotic mop, are two examples of consumer products that people can purchase to help clean their homes. But a hospital needs a more heavy-duty cleaning machine. Intellibot robots scrub, vacuum, or sweep floors in hospitals and other large buildings. They do this automatically, so cleaning staff do not have to spend all day pushing heavy mopping machines around. At Kapi'olani Medical Center for Women & Children in Hawaii, a pair of Intellibot machines were decorated to resemble a train and a school bus. "Beyond freeing up the cleaning crew so they can focus on keeping the environment as safe and clean as possible, the robots are putting a smile on the faces of their patients," says Thomas Boscher of Intellibot Robotics.[20]

Mopping robots clean a floor with soap and water in much the same way that a human would. But when it comes to disinfecting tables, door handles, toilet seats, medical equipment, and other surfaces in hospital rooms, robots have an advantage.

First Robotic Hospital

At Humber River Hospital in Toronto, Canada, pharmacy robots mix drugs and courier robots scurry around, transporting supplies. Robotic beds can automatically position patients. But these machines aren't the only robotic aspect of the hospital. The entire building is connected digitally. Hospital workers and patients wear tracking devices, making it possible to always know where a particular person is. Using bedside touchscreen interfaces, patients can video chat with their doctors, access their electronic health records, order food, or read e-books. In a way the hospital is like one huge robot. "Humber is the first hospital in North America to have all of its systems electronic and integrated together," says CEO Dr. Reuben Devlin.

Quoted in MEDITECH, "Humber River Hospital Opens North America's First Fully Digital Hospital," October 27, 2015. https://ehr.meditech.com.

They can use ultraviolet (UV) light. This high-energy light destroys DNA, which is an essential part of the cells of all living things. UV light zaps dangerous bacteria that are gathered on surfaces or even floating in the air. Since UV light harms humans, too, a person can't safely use this method to clean a room. But robots that clean with UV light abound, including Xenex, Tru-D, and UV-Disinfection Robot.

ultraviolet

light with a very short wavelength that is damaging to living cells

In most hospitals these robots do not replace human workers, but instead add an extra layer of protection against dangerous germs. Human workers follow the usual routine of removing linens and trash from a room, then wiping down surfaces using chemical cleaning spray and a cloth. The robot comes in afterward to sanitize any areas the human may have missed. The robots are especially important in the areas of a hospital where patients are at the highest risk of acquiring an infection, including burn units, intensive care units, and operating rooms. "The robot gives us one more tool in the arsenal," says Debbie Sandberg of Sutter Health Medical Center in California, which uses a Xenex robot that the staff named Xhaiden. "People want to know they're in a clean environment. This gives everyone more confidence from a patient-safety perspective."[21] Several hospitals have reported that health care–associated infection rates dropped significantly after they added UV-disinfecting robots to their cleaning routines.

Dispensing Drugs

In addition to combating health care–associated infections, robots could help eliminate medication errors. If a patient takes the wrong medicine, an incorrect dose, or a problematic combination of drugs, his or her health may suffer. This is called an adverse drug event, and it usually happens due to human error in dispensing or delivering prescription medications. A pharmacist is the person tasked with preparing doses of medication for patients. A 2012 study in the *American Journal of Health-System Pharmacy* found that a human pharmacist makes an average of five errors in every

A pharmacy robot in a hospital counts pills and selects medicines for patients. The robot can fill six prescriptions at a time, making sure patients are getting the right medications and the proper doses.

100,000 orders filled. Robots are perfectly suited to the repetitive tasks of pill grabbing and pill counting—they don't get bored, distracted, or tired. As a result robot pharmacists are much more accurate than humans. After the PillPick robot pharmacy system came online in 2011 at the UCSF Medical Center, it filled 350,000 orders without a single error.

Robot pharmacies are typically custom-built to fit the needs of the medical facility. Often as large as a closet or a small room, the robots are basically smart vending machines. "The hulking room-sized machine . . . was a labyrinth of rubber conveyor belts, miles of pneumatic pipes, and finely calibrated, suction-powered, pill-picking arms," wrote journalist Farhad Manjoo after watching the UCSF robot in action.[22] All human workers have to do is load in trays or boxes of medications to keep the robot stocked. As each prescription comes in, the robot checks the patient's records, selects and counts pills, and then prepares and labels a custom package of medication to be delivered to the patient.

labyrinth

a complicated maze

Mark Laret of the UCSF Medical Center believes the hospital's $7 million investment in the PillPick robot was good for everybody. He says, "The pharmacists got out of doing work that was menial for them, and it allowed the machines to do what they do best, which is accurately count pills. . . . The machine counts pills much better than humans do."[23] The human pharmacists now spend their time going on rounds with doctors and nurses to discuss medications with patients.

Not all medication comes in easily countable pill form, however. Some drugs must be injected using a syringe, and other medicines are administered directly into a patient's veins from an IV bag. These medicines must be carefully mixed and measured in a sterile environment. The RIVA automated compounding system is designed specifically to fill syringes or IV bags. Thom Doherty of Intelligent Hospital Systems was one of the engineers who designed RIVA. He says, "My background is in aerospace. . . . Our joke was that IV automation is like rocket science, but hard. For example, one of our customers identified 42 separate steps that you need to make a single syringe."[24]

A Mars Rover on Earth

On the planet Mars, the robot *Curiosity* drives across the dusty terrain, sampling rocks and taking pictures. The same types of systems that allow this space-faring robot to navigate also propel hospital robots. As a graduate student at MIT in the late 1990s, Daniel Theobald worked on a prototype of a rover that might be used to explore another planet. He focused on developing an operating system that would give the robot autonomy to plan its own path from place to place. Later, Theobald joined the robotics company Vecna Technologies. He realized the work he had done with space exploration robots had other potential applications. "I thought, if we can successfully have a robot operate on Mars for an extended period of time, then we should have robots on Earth, providing value on a daily basis," he says. Vecna produced QC Bot, a mobile robot that delivers items in a hospital. Theobald explains that the hospital robot has several things in common with a Mars rover. "Like the Mars rover," he continues, "it must be able to operate robustly in a complex, unstructured environment away from the engineers who designed and built it."

Quoted in NASA *Spinoff*, "Rovers Pave the Way for Hospital Robots," 2012. https://spinoff.nasa.gov.

Robotics technology can also help mix chemotherapy drugs, a special class of medication used to treat cancer. During chemotherapy treatment, a patient will go in for lab work, then wait as a doctor reviews those lab results and orders an individualized mix of drugs based on that information. As chemotherapy drugs are very toxic, humans must take special precautions while handling them. Robots can handle the drugs safely and with more precision than human workers. They can also help speed up the process. The Apoteca chemotherapy robot can prepare up to twelve individualized doses per hour, three times as many as a human technician, according to the University of Maryland's Marlene and Stewart Greenebaum Comprehensive Cancer Center.

Medical staff must take extraordinary precautions when handling chemotherapy medicines because the drugs involved can be fatal to humans. Robots can select, mix, and package these toxic drugs without worry.

Robots can also assist with inserting a needle into a vein. Veebot is a robotic arm that automates the process of drawing blood or inserting an IV line. The robot finds the best vein to puncture 83 percent of the time, which is about as good as a human nurse. The company Vasculogic is working on a competing design called VenousPro. They report that their system achieved 97 percent accuracy in choosing a good puncture site. But both robots will still have to overcome human fears about getting stuck with a needle. Richard Harris, founder and chief executive officer (CEO) of Veebot, asserts, "We believe if this machine works better, faster, and cheaper than a person, people will want to use it."[25]

Robots that assist with preparing and administering medication, delivering supplies, and cleaning rooms do the mundane, taken-for-granted jobs, ensuring that a hospital runs smoothly. While these robots may not seem as exciting as an automated surgical system or a humanoid nurse, they are just as important to the future of health care.

CHAPTER 4

Diagnosis, Care, and Treatment

Robots are gradually becoming competent enough to take over medical tasks such as basic patient care, patient consultations, and disease diagnosis. Using robots can allow a doctor or nurse to interact with many more patients than they normally could. In addition, computer algorithms armed with artificial intelligence can augment a doctor's mind, making it possible to perform diagnoses with more accuracy than usual. Finally, some nursing robots combine body and mind, providing both a physical presence and companionship to patients.

Could robots ever completely replace human doctors and nurses? Most experts think that there will always be a human component to medicine. "I don't think computers will ever supplant the doctor's diagnosis. I think things will change. . . . A computer may become a second opinion, or perhaps even a first opinion, but the doctor will still make the final call," says Richard Lilford, a professor at the University of Warwick in England.[26] Robots likely will never be able to listen to their patients or care about them in the same way another human being does. Whether or not robotics technology ever replaces doctors and nurses, it is certainly changing the way people interact with their caregivers.

A Virtual Body

At St. Charles Medical Center–Redmond in Oregon, a doctor's face peers out from a video screen attached to a robot body. He asks a nurse to place a stethoscope against a patient's chest. The stethoscope is linked to the robot and transmits its sound to the doctor's headphones. The doctor is in a different city, but he is able to perform an entire patient assessment thanks to the nurse and the telepresence robot, which the staff has nicknamed "Roda." The robot's official name is RP-7, and it debuted in 2008. InTouch Health, the company that makes RP-7, estimates that seventy thousand doctor-patient sessions are conducted using the robot each year.

Of course, basic telepresence does not require a robot. Communications technology has advanced to the point where most cell phones come equipped with the ability to make video calls.

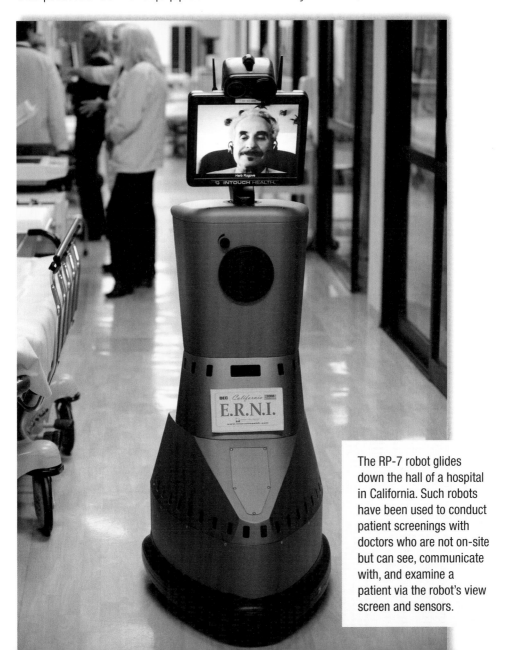

The RP-7 robot glides down the hall of a hospital in California. Such robots have been used to conduct patient screenings with doctors who are not on-site but can see, communicate with, and examine a patient via the robot's view screen and sensors.

But pairing video calls with a robot allows the physician to move around and interact more naturally with a patient.

A doctor has to navigate RP-7 from place to place with a joystick. But InTouch Health's newest robot can navigate on its own. The company partnered with iRobot, known for its vacuum cleaning and mopping robots, to release the RP-VITA (Remote Presence Virtual + Independent Telemedicine Assistant) in 2014. To maneuver this model, a doctor uses an iPad to tap on a location on a map of the hospital. Then the robot navigates there on its own. Yulun Wang, CEO of InTouch, the company that makes RP-VITA, says, "We want to enable the clinician to be able to be present somewhere else—from anywhere to anywhere—and operate and work as if they were standing there in person."[27] Giraff AB, VGo, and SAM are other brands of telepresence robots being used in hospitals and other medical practices.

Some telepresence robots incorporate arms, allowing them to accomplish tasks other than just communicating. One example is TRINA, short for Tele-Robotic Intelligent Nursing Assistant. It can deliver a cup, bowl, or pills using its arms. The National Science Foundation funded the robot, which is still under development. "We need to establish a better interface with the human and the robot to make them work together and be more comfortable," says Jianqiao Li, a student at Duke University who is working on the robot.[28] QC Bot and some other courier robots also come with basic telepresence abilities.

interface

a connection between two systems

Using one of these robots, a primary care doctor can make house calls in the middle of the night or at patients' homes without having to go anywhere. A specialist in a rare condition can easily consult with patients all over the world. An infectious disease specialist can assist people during a deadly outbreak without putting on protective gear. The robot acts as a virtual body for the doctor, allowing him or her to interact with patients without actually traveling anywhere.

A Robotic Mind

A doctor who consults with patients using a robotic body and a video screen probably doesn't seem that unusual. A human doc-

Go Team, Go!

At Dartmouth College in New Hampshire, the football team has welcomed a new assistant, a VGo robot. This telepresence robot rolls around on wheels bearing a video screen at the top of a long, slender body. VGo traveled with the team to all its games throughout 2014. When a football player got hit in the head, the robot connected to a neurosurgeon at Dartmouth-Hitchcock Medical Center who would assess the player for a concussion. "By partnering with the Dartmouth-Hitchcock Center for Telehealth we can tap into the latest technology and provide additional medical coverage by having a neurosurgeon on call should a player suffer a significant head injury or need a concussion screening," says Drew Galbraith of Dartmouth College.

Quoted in Dartmouth-Hitchcock Office of Communications & Marketing, "Telemedicine Robot to Roam the Football Sidelines this Fall," Dartmouth Big Green, September 18, 2014. www.dartmouthsports.com.

tor is still the one performing the assessment and diagnosis. But medical technology can assist with these more cerebral tasks as well, effectively extending a doctor's mind. Artificial intelligence (AI) algorithms diagnose diseases, suggest treatments, and even assist with medical research. Although these computer intelligences do not have bodies, some call them robots because they are smart machines made to assist humans.

Watson, the AI program built by IBM that defeated human *Jeopardy!* champions, has done more for health care than just giving the robot MERA a voice. IBM has been training the program to analyze medical information in order to assist with cancer diagnoses. "Determining the right drug combination for an advanced cancer patient is alarmingly difficult," says Norman Sharpless, a doctor and director of the University of North Carolina's Lineberger Cancer Center.[29] Cancer is not really one disease but a suite of different conditions that all require different treatment approaches. The traditional treatments of surgery, chemotherapy, and radiation work for many cancers but not all. Researchers are learning how to target cancer cells more specifically by analyzing a patient's genetics. But sorting through the genetic information for a single person can take a team of human experts hours, days, or even weeks. Watson can perform the task in minutes.

In addition to understanding the patient's unique form of cancer, a doctor also has to stay up-to-date on the latest medical research, including scientific studies, clinical trials, and medical records. Human doctors simply do not have time to read through every single piece of information related to a patient's case. But Watson does. The AI program accesses the latest data on cancer treatment and uses it to compare treatment options. In a test of Watson's abilities, researchers provided the computer with one thousand cancer cases. Watson recommended the same treatment as human doctors in 99 percent of those cases.

In one real case in Japan in 2016, Watson correctly diagnosed a woman with a rare form of leukemia, and doctors quickly switched her to a better treatment plan. "It might be an exaggeration to say AI saved her life, but it surely gave us the data we needed in an extremely speedy fashion," says Arinobu Tojo, a professor at the University of Tokyo's Institute of Medical Science.[30] Without Watson, the woman would have had to wait two weeks for human experts to sort through her genetic data. "Watson fills in for some human limitations," says Marty Kohn, an emergency room doctor who was part of the IBM team that trained Watson to perform diagnoses. Humans just aren't good at carefully perusing large amounts of information. Kohn says, "That's where Watson shines: taking a huge list of information and winnowing it down."[31]

Artificial intelligence is assisting in other areas of diagnosis and treatment as well. Medical devices have used algorithms to recognize patterns in data for a long time—for example, to detect a heart problem in an electrocardiogram, which is a graph of the heart's electrical activity. But these algorithms rely on set rules. New artificial intelligence software allows medical algorithms to learn from experience. The more examples of a disease the algorithm sees, the more accurately it will diagnose the disease in the future. In 2015 researchers at Stanford University in California used a machine learning algorithm to look at images of moles, rashes, and other marks on the skin and pick out cases of skin cancer. In tests the algorithm exceeded human doctors' performance at distinguishing cancerous marks from benign ones. The researchers hope that software such as this will offer people an easy, inexpensive way to screen themselves for skin cancer at home. Similar AI algorithms have been developed to detect breast cancer, lung disease, heart disease, and more. The role of radiologists, human specialists who look at medical images to find problematic areas, will have to change. "It's just completely obvious that in five years deep learning is going to do better than radiologists [at detecting disease]," says Geoffrey Hinton, an AI expert at the University of Toronto in Canada.[32]

In the future, smart diagnostic systems could continually monitor people for disease, according to Sebastian Thrun, an AI expert at Stanford University. Thrun imagines cell phones that analyze their users' speech for signs of dementia, steering wheels that detect hand tremors as a sign of Parkinson's disease, and a bathtub that uses ultrasound scanning to check internal organs for tumors. "The cognitive revolution will allow computers to amplify the capacity of the human mind," Thrun

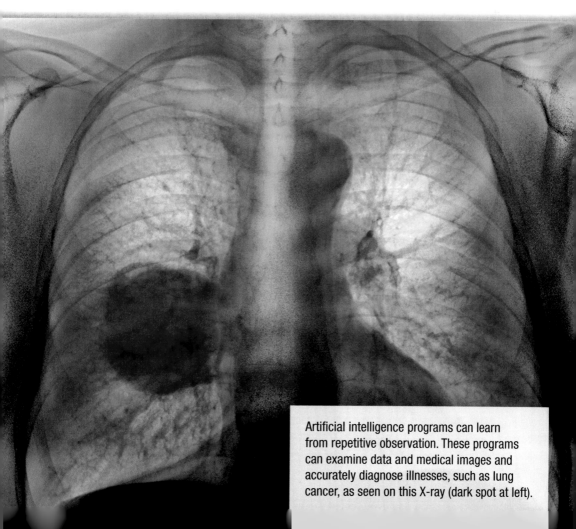

Artificial intelligence programs can learn from repetitive observation. These programs can examine data and medical images and accurately diagnose illnesses, such as lung cancer, as seen on this X-ray (dark spot at left).

asserts. "Just as machines made human muscles a thousand times stronger, machines will make the human brain a thousand times more powerful."[33]

Call the Carebot

People do not just want smart doctors; they want caring doctors. To a patient, a doctor's or a nurse's compassion, patience, and friendliness may be more important than that caretaker's diagnostic accuracy or efficiency. However, the world is facing a shortage of humans to provide this type of companionship, especially to growing populations of elderly people. The race is on to develop a nursing robot—also called a "carebot"—that would combine physical care with emotional care. The ultimate carebot would be able to assist an elderly or disabled person with a range of daily tasks, including getting in and out of bed, eating, bathing, remembering to take medicine or check vital signs, and sending an alarm in case of an emergency. In addition to practical assistance, the ideal carebot should also offer companionship and entertainment.

Medical Research

Watson and other AI programs churn through the latest medical research in order to make a diagnosis. Some of that medical research is also the result of smart robots or algorithms at work. In fact, AI promises to completely transform the field of drug development. Currently, it takes around fifteen years and $1 billion to bring a new drug to market. When a company begins to develop a new drug, it must test thousands of compounds against each other to figure out how they interact. An AI system called AtomNet can test 1 million compounds every day, a task that would take a human team months. Another system tests combinations of cancer drugs to see how effective they might be. "We have built a robot system that plans and conducts experiments with many substances, and draws its own conclusions from the results," says Claes Andersson of Uppsala University in Sweden. AI technology promises to shorten the length of time and reduce the amount of money it takes for drug companies to identify possible new drugs, develop them, and test them.

Quoted in Uppsala Universitet, "New Smart Robot Accelerates Cancer Treatment Research," ScienceDaily, September 22, 2015. www.sciencedaily.com.

However, no carebot today can accomplish all of these things. Nursing robots typically focus on just a few of these tasks. Some are like animated virtual assistants, tasked with providing reminders and information to the user. Pearl, released in 2000 as one of the earliest carebots, provides reminders throughout the day. "She tries to figure out if the person has done what she's supposed to do and, if not, remind her to do it," says Martha Pollack, a professor of electrical engineering at the University of Michigan.[34] Pollack was part of a team that tested Pearl with residents in a retirement home in 2004. The Mabu robot is a more recent example of this type of health care assistant. Mabu looks like a tablet with a yellow robot head attached. Its main job is to remind elderly people to take their medication throughout the day, but it can also hold conversations. IBM's MERA is another example of a carebot focused on reminders and conversation. MERA, however, can also monitor its patients for falls and send an alert in case of an emergency.

Pepper, the robot body that MERA uses, has also found work as a guide, answering questions at shopping malls, restaurants, and on cruise ships. In 2016 two hospitals in Belgium added Pepper robots to the reception area of the hospital. When Pepper sees a person who might need help, it moves its head and gestures with its arms as it says, "Hello, I am Pepper. Can I help you with something?"[35] The robot can say phrases like this in nineteen languages and can also help show people how to get to different parts of the hospital.

However, Pepper was designed to do more than just provide reminders or guide people. The Japanese company SoftBank Robotics developed Pepper to be a likable, humanoid companion. Pepper is the size of a human child, with humanlike arms, a cartoony head and face, and a computer screen in its chest. It rolls around on wheels hidden beneath a flat base. In Japanese homes, seven thousand of the robots answer questions, greet guests, and play with kids. "We designed Pepper's form to incentivize engagement," says Steve Carlin of SoftBank Robotics. "Its height, shape, the fact that it has arms that can gesticulate—are all designed

gesticulate

to make motions with the hands or arms in order to add meaning to speech to show empathy."[36] The robot even uses artificial intelligence to recognize the emotions conveyed in human facial expressions and respond accordingly. In addition SoftBank Robotics is working on making Pepper aware of its user's cultural background. The robot will eventually be able to alter its interactions to fit the customs and etiquette of the user.

Robot Companions

Pepper is one of many carebots that focus on companionship. Also called social robots, these machines are designed to interact fluidly with people in order to inspire trust and keep the user engaged. Many social robots look humanoid and use human gestures and expressions in order to make interaction feel more natural. Toshiba's ChihiraAico and Actroid F are both robot bodies designed to look as human as possible. The effect is very lifelike, but some find it creepy. Most social robots are designed to look like friendly machines rather than people. Examples include Pepper, Honda's ASIMO, Tico, and iCub, all similar in size to a human child; Nao, a doll-sized social robot; and Kirobo, which is even tinier, at just 4 inches (10 cm) tall. All could potentially become important companions and assistants in the health care industry. But these robots only work as well as the software that controls their bodies and powers their communication abilities. A social robot is a high-tech platform, like a cell phone or a tablet. The role it performs depends on the applications engineers write for it.

Nao, especially, has become a popular platform for health care and therapy applications. At the Hospital San Raffaele in Italy, researchers are testing Nao's ability to cheer up kids who have diabetes. Likewise, a husband and wife research team based in Connecticut has developed software for Nao aimed at handling some of the ethical dilemmas that nurses regularly face. For example, if a patient refuses to take medication, this robot balances the amount of harm that might befall the patient from missing a dose against that patient's right to make his or her own choices. Based on this comparison, the robot will decide whether to do nothing, wait and try again a little while later, or alert a doctor.

ASK Nao, short for Autism Solution for Kids, is software that gives the robot the ability to play educational games with children. "[They] work on verbal and non-verbal communication, emotional intelligence, mimicking, and even basic academic skills," says Olivier Joubert of Aldebaran, the company that makes Nao. Kaspar, an entirely different social robot, was specially designed to assist children with autism. One boy, for example, who struggles with

The miniature NAO robot has been designed to move like a human and interact with people it meets. Here, a NAO robot helps cheer up residents in a nursing home by talking, singing, dancing, and even leading exercise classes.

anxiety issues, was having trouble eating with other children in his class. His school principal, Alice Lynch, says, "We started [working] with Kaspar and [the student] really, really enjoyed feeding Kaspar, making him eat when he was hungry, things like that. Now he's started to integrate into the classroom and eat alongside his peers."[37] Bandit and Cosmobot are two more examples of social robots designed to assist children with special needs.

The company ZoraBots has developed software that turns either the Pepper or Nao robot into a lively, interactive companion for the elderly or for children. With Zora software, the Nao robot can lead a physical therapy class, read news or weather forecasts, or even get people dancing. Fabrice Goffin, one of the creators of Zora, says that the robot could help people feel less lonely. "Solitude is something which is horrible for a lot of elderly people. People don't have all the time to visit their families and they can find some kind of relationship with the robot and that is a nice thing to do," he says.[38]

A robot doesn't have to look humanoid to offer companionship. Paro, a robot designed to resemble a baby seal, is a stuffed animal endowed with artificial intelligence that allows it to respond to people's voices and touch. Research has shown that playing with Paro can calm and comfort elderly patients with dementia. One woman who had a chance to interact with the robot remarked, "I know you're not real. But somehow, I don't know, I love you."[39] Companies including Sony and Hasbro have also released robot pets in the forms of cats, dogs, and other cuddly creatures, and some facilities have incorporated the toys into elder care programs. Many experts argue that "robotherapy" is similar to pet therapy, in which living animals are brought into nursing homes to keep residents company and boost their moods. Some people form relationships with companion robots that feel as real as the relationship with a living cat or dog.

A Human Touch

On the other hand, some experts find the idea of robotic nurses, doctors, and companions to be unsettling or even disturbing. "Isn't it a shame that with all the people in the world we haven't got enough nurses," states Rodney Bickerstaffe of the National Pensioners Convention. "It's a bit dehumanising and I think personal care and human touch is what it's about."[40] Sherry Turkle, a social scientist at the Massachusetts Institute of Technology (MIT), worries that companion robots like Paro could trick vulnerable patients into caring about something that will never care back. She believes that technology can never replace a real-life relationship with a human being. But the sad truth is that there likely won't be enough human health care professionals to go around in the near future. "A reliable robot may be better than an unreliable or abusive person, or than no one at all," says Louise Aronson, an expert in elder care at the University of California, San Francisco.[41] She has cared for many elderly patients and imagines that their lives could only be improved by having a robot nearby all day and night to talk to and interact with.

Thankfully, both medical and robotics experts agree that robotics technology is not intended to take over health care from humans. Rather, robotics and artificial intelligence add to doctors' and caregivers' abilities, allowing them to know more and accomplish more than they could previously. "It's really not about replacing [doctors and nurses], but augmenting them so they can ultimately do a better job at managing a large number of patients," says Cory Kidd of Catalia Health, maker of the Mabu robot.[42] And who knows, perhaps robots will one day become smart enough to truly care about their patients.

CHAPTER 5

From Therapy to Cyborgs

In addition to reminding patients about medication and other scheduled events and providing companionship and support, human nurses and caretakers spend a lot of time helping elderly or disabled patients accomplish daily tasks. Depending on the patient's condition, a nurse may have to feed the person, bathe him or her, fetch items the person wants, or help the person move from place to place. Robotics technology can assist with all of these tasks, making the nurse's job less strenuous. In some cases a robot or bionic body part can eliminate the need for a human caretaker entirely.

Some robotics technology even becomes part of a patient's body. Exoskeletons and bionic limbs can restore independence to patients who are unable to use their own arms or legs. They can also enhance a healthy person's strength or turn a person into a cyborg—an individual with both biological and mechanical body parts.

Lifting and Moving

Riken, a government-backed research institute in Japan, has developed a series of robot bears designed to help lift and move people. Nursing staff must lift patients out of bed, into wheelchairs or walkers, and then back into bed dozens of times every day. As a result, nursing assistants are more likely than any other occupation to suffer from back problems, according to the US Bureau of Labor Statistics. Some hospitals have installed mechanical lifts that nursing staff can use to move patients, but these lifts are often installed in the ceiling or are large and cumbersome to move from place to place. A robot could make the lifting process faster, easier, and more enjoyable for both the patient and the assistants.

Riken's latest lifting robot, Robear, stands as tall as an average human adult and weighs approximately 300 pounds (140 kg). Robear has long, padded arms, a cute, cartoon-bear face, and rolls around on wheels. The robot can turn patients in bed who cannot turn over by themselves, lift patients out of bed, and then help them stand and walk or sit in a wheelchair. RoNA, short for Robotic Nursing Assistant, is a similar system that also has

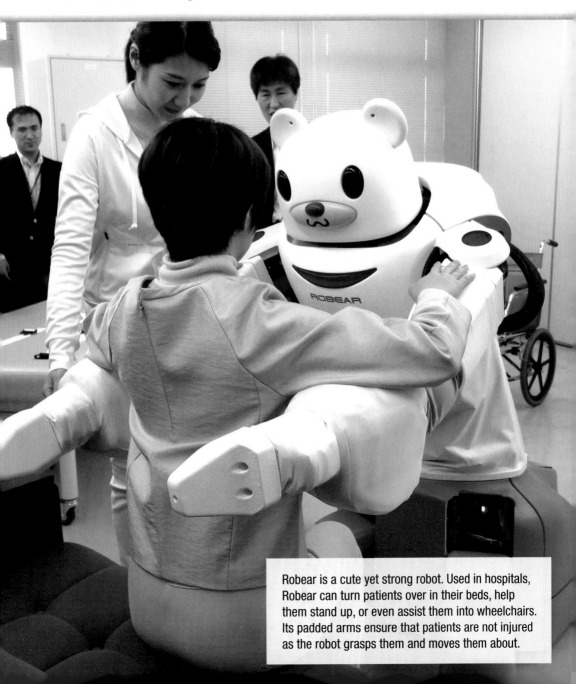

Robear is a cute yet strong robot. Used in hospitals, Robear can turn patients over in their beds, help them stand up, or even assist them into wheelchairs. Its padded arms ensure that patients are not injured as the robot grasps them and moves them about.

long arms and a smiling face. Some robotic lifting devices have a more practical design. Robohelper Sasuke is a robotic system that looks like a sling attached to a mechanical base, and it helps a patient transition from sitting to standing. It can be paired with a device called Robohelper Love, which is a cup that fits like underwear and can automatically sense urine or feces. Hoses attached to the cup remove the waste, and then the system cleans the patient.

Other robotic devices try to eliminate the need to move people from one device to another. The Panasonic Resyone is a bed that converts into a wheelchair. And the Yurina is a nursing robot that performs a number of functions. Its main body looks similar to Robear or RoNA—with a rolling base, a computer-screen face, and long arms—but the arms attach to a bed that folds into a chair. A patient can operate the robot independently using a controller or voice commands. "This robot is actually used in an Osaka hospital," says Yoshitaka Takata of Japan Logic Machine, the company that makes Yurina. "It can lift people from beds and carry them to other places. It can also help people take baths and change diapers. So this robot can be used for quite a lot of care tasks that require physical strength."[43]

Wheelchairs are also getting smarter and more adaptable thanks to robotics. A new wheelchair system designed by researchers at MIT can learn to find its own way around a building as well as how to respond to its user's preferred commands. When the user first brings the wheelchair home, he or she simply has to drive it around, telling it what each room is called. Then all the user has to do is say, "Take me to the kitchen," or "Go to my room," and the wheelchair will know where to go. "It's a system that can learn and adapt to the user," says Nicholas Roy of MIT.[44] The wheelchair is now being tested at a nursing home in Massachusetts with real patients.

Another robotic wheelchair, developed at the Chiba Institute of Technology in Japan, can step over obstacles or climb stairs. The chair has four wheels attached to robotic legs. When sensors on the legs detect a step or other object in the way, the robot positions its legs for stability, then lifts one up and over. It can also line up its wheels and use stabilizers in order to spin in a circle. The seat of the chair tilts in order to keep the user level as the robot steps up stairs or rolls down a ramp. The iBot, which debuted in 2003, was one of the first wheelchairs to offer users the ability to climb stairs. The wheels could stack one on top of the other to go up or down steps or to allow the user to come up to other people's eye level. "When you go out to a social setting, back up at 6 feet, talking to somebody eye to eye, you get this sense of dignity. The disability just kind of fades into the background," says iBot user Gary Linfoot.[45]

Exoskeletons

Smarter wheelchairs are a great advancement, but another new technology promises to allow many people who currently use wheelchairs to walk instead. An exoskeleton is a robotic suit that enhances the wearer's strength and physical ability. It may fit over the entire body, or just over one or more limbs.

These devices are most commonly used for rehabilitating people who have been injured in an accident or weakened by an illness such as a stroke. Many victims of strokes end up partially paralyzed, unable to fully move their limbs. In physical therapy, patients perform repetitive motions, usually with the help of a human therapist, to regain strength and mobility. Robotic devices

A Real Iron Man

Exoskeletons and bionic implants have been developed to restore normal mobility to people with physical limitations. But these devices could also amplify the abilities of healthy individuals, just like the comic book character Iron Man, who gets his superpowers from a bionic suit. The company Panasonic has developed a bionic suit called the Ninja that is intended to help people lift heavy boxes or climb steep mountains. And the US Department of Defense is working on Iron Man–style suits for military use. The XOS 2 suit, demonstrated in 2010, allows wearers to easily lift 200 pounds (91 kg) again and again without tiring. Enhancements such as these bring up serious ethical questions, however. One day, people might elect to modify their own bodies in order to become better, stronger, and faster than everyone else. This could create a distinct class division between those who can afford the enhancements and those who cannot. A real-life Iron Man could easily take advantage of normal humans. But this type of troubling situation is still a long way off, since bionic parts are not yet functional enough for healthy people to get any benefit from using them routinely.

can help improve the experience. The therapist's job becomes less physically demanding, and the patient can avoid constant visits to a clinic by using one of these devices at home. HARMONY is one example of a two-armed exoskeleton that fits over a patient's arms and upper body and can guide a patient through a full range of natural motion. ADLER, short for Activities of Daily Living Exercise Robot, looks more like an industrial robot arm. It grasps a patient's hand and wrist and moves the arm through motions such as drinking from a cup or combing the hair. Once the patient's original range of motion has been restored, physical therapy robots are no longer needed.

For people who are paralyzed, though, exoskeletons could become a part of daily life. The robots can manipulate immobile arms or legs through the motions necessary to reach for objects or even walk. In 2014 the ReWalk became the first exoskeleton approved by the FDA for personal use. The device fits over a person's legs like a brace, but contains sensors and motors that propel the legs. Someone who is paralyzed from the waist down can use ReWalk to stand up, walk, or even climb stairs. Stacey Kozal of Ohio used a similar exoskeleton device, called the Ottobock C-Brace, to hike the Appalachian Trail. ReWalk user Paul Jenkins of Australia says, "Some people completely ignore your existence when you're in a chair . . . in the exoskeleton people look at you differently straight away. One of the first things you notice is a lot more people smile at you."[46] Other exoskeletons available to paralyzed people include the SuitX Phoenix, Ekso GT, and Indego. Unfortunately, these devices are extremely expensive, and health insurance often doesn't cover the cost. A ReWalk device costs $70,000 or more, while the Indego exoskeleton is over $90,000 and cannot climb stairs.

For a paralyzed patient, an exoskeleton must provide rigid support and do all of the work of walking. As a result these suits are usually quite heavy. But elderly people or adults and children with movement disorders, including multiple sclerosis, usually retain some ability to move their own limbs. They just need some extra help. Engineers are developing more-comfortable, lightweight exosuits using soft robotics technology. The company ReWalk is working with the Wyss Institute in Massachusetts on a soft exo-suit product called the Restore. A suit like this would more closely resemble clothing than machinery. Conor Walsh of the Wyss Institute describes his team's suit as "soft wearable robots that act in parallel with the body's muscles and tendons and mimic their function."[47] He says that the suit could assist anyone who needs extra strength, including people with physical disabilities as well as healthy individuals who are performing difficult work.

The ReWalk exoskeleton helps keep a paralyzed patient stable as he or she learns to walk for the first time or walk again after an injury. The unit's motors move paralyzed limbs to give the wearer greater freedom of movement.

New Arms and Legs

Patients who use exoskeletons already have arms and legs of their own. But amputees are missing one or more limbs and may need a new body part called a prosthesis. Basic wooden or metal prostheses have been around since ancient times, but these devices could not grasp or move like a real arm or leg.

One problem with early mechanical prosthetic legs was the knee joint. A simple hinge could not adjust to different gaits, such as walking and running. A person using such a knee would walk with an awkward gait. As computers became more advanced and shrank in size during the late 1980s, engineers started adding microprocessors to knee joints. A microprocessor is a computer tiny enough to fit on a single chip. The Intelligent Knee, developed at the Kobe Steel Company in Japan during this time, was the first to use this technology inside the joint of an artificial leg. The C-leg, developed in the early 1990s by Kelly James of the University of Alberta in Canada, soon followed. Ottobock, the same company that now makes C-braces, launched the C-leg as a commercial product in 1999. David Boone of OrthoCare Innovations recalls watching a person run on a treadmill using a prosthesis with a computer-controlled knee. The person was "transitioning seamlessly from a slow walk to a fast run and back again."[48] The tiny computer inside adjusted the timing of each swing of the leg to match the user's pace. Many leg prostheses today incorporate similar technology into the ankles as well.

Prosthetic arms present an even greater challenge to roboticists. "Human standing and walking are kind of rhythmic activities that are easier to program and control," says Robert Jaeger, of the Veterans Health Administration Office of Research & Development. "But with an arm, you have a whole host of things you may want to manipulate that cannot possibly be programmed into the device."[49] These activities include eating, drinking, shaking hands, opening doors, cooking, driving, and more. Hook-style prosthetic arms, like the one sported by Captain Hook in the story *Peter Pan*, were once the standard. But robotic arms and hands with fingers that move like a real human limb are becoming more common. For a prosthetic arm to truly take the place of a real arm, it must provide a natural range of motion as well as intuitive controls.

In the *Star Wars* movies, Luke Skywalker loses his hand and receives a new robotic one that functions just as well as his old hand did. The "Luke Arm" got its nickname thanks to the *Star Wars* movies. Officially called the DEKA arm, it received FDA approval in 2014. Inventor Dean Kamen developed the arm with funding from DARPA. "This prosthetic limb system can pick up objects as delicate as a grape, as well [as] being able to handle very rugged tools like a hand drill," says Justin Sanchez of DARPA.[50] Variations on the arm include the entire arm and shoulder, the elbow and hand, or the hand only.

The i-limb series of bionic hands offers similar functionality. Both the DEKA arm and i-limb hand contain sensors that detect muscle twitches in the user's remaining arm or shoulder. These twitches get converted into commands that tell the arm how to move or change its grip. Users can also change the limb's settings using foot pads or even a digital app. With the i-limb, users can also gesture with the hand to change its grip. Sixteen-year-old Patrick Kane received an i-limb in 2013. "It's not so much

Nine-year-old Josh Cathcart demonstrates a robotic i-limb that replaced his lost right hand. Such robotic devices are lightweight and agile, allowing recipients to easily grasp and manipulate objects.

that it allows me to do new things but it will allow me to do things more smoothly and naturally," he says.[51] Touch Bionics, maker of the i-limb, also offers i-digits for people who are missing fingers. Thanks to all of these advances in robotic limbs, Jaeger says, "there is talk of no longer speaking of prosthetic arms but of wearable robotic devices because today's prostheses are increasingly more robotic."[52]

Becoming Cyborgs

Luke Skywalker did not have to gesture or manipulate foot sensors to use his robotic hand. He could move the hand naturally and feel sensations through it. Engineers are developing interfaces for robotic limbs that connect directly to a user's nerves or brain. These interfaces allow a user to move a robotic limb using thoughts or even to feel sensations through robotic skin.

There are two ways to give a person mind control over a bionic part. The first is targeted muscle reinnervation (TMR). This procedure involves rewiring the nervous system. Nerves that used to carry brain instructions to the missing arm and hand muscles get reattached to muscles that are still there. In 2001 Todd Kuiken's team at the Rehabilitation Institute of Chicago performed TMR surgery on Jesse Sullivan, who had lost both arms in an electrical accident. Sullivan became the first person to control a robotic arm with his mind. When he decides to open his robotic hand, for example, his brain sends a signal through the hand nerve, which is now attached to a muscle in his chest. The chest muscle contracts, which signals the bionic hand to open. But from Sullivan's point of view, "All I have to do is want to do it, and I do it," he says.[53] Amanda Kitts went through the same procedure in 2007. She used to have to flex certain muscles in her back and biceps to move her robotic wrist or elbow, which was too slow and tedious to be really useful to her. With the new system, she says, "I'm able to move my hand, wrist and

targeted muscle reinnervation

a procedure in which nerves that used to travel to a missing limb are rerouted to connect to working muscles in order to control a prosthetic device elbow all at the same time. You think, and then your muscles move."[54] TMR has been used to help amputees control bionic legs as well. Kuiken's team pioneered the first mind-controlled leg in 2010.

Messages from nerves travel the other way, too—back up to the brain, carrying touch sensations. Dustin J. Tyler of Case Western Reserve University explains that most people think about how an amputee has lost the function of the missing limb. But sensation is just as important. "That is probably the thing that makes us human," he says. "[Touch] is the piece that connects us to the world around us and it's the piece that connects us to other people."[55]

After Sullivan had been using his robotic arms for a few months, Kuiken noticed something strange. When a doctor or nurse touched Sullivan's chest, he felt it in his fingers or thumb. "He feels hot, cold, sharp, dull, all in his missing hand, or both his hand and his chest, but he can attend to either," says Kuiken.[56] Many research groups are working on ways to restore touch sensation to amputees. Tyler's team has developed pressure sensors for a robotic hand that connect to electrodes wrapped around the outside of an amputee's arm stump. The electrodes send touch sensations from the hand and into the nerves, which carry them to the brain, allowing the user to feel pressure and

Mind Control

Jan Scheuermann, who is paralyzed from the neck down, had electrodes implanted in her brain in 2012 to see if she could learn to move a robotic arm with her thoughts. "I had been a quadriplegic for 12 years," she says. "I hadn't moved anything. . . . I was determined I was going to move that robotic arm." In a series of experiments with researchers at the University of Pittsburgh in Pennsylvania, Scheuermann picked up and moved objects, opened a door, and fed herself a chocolate bar. "It was the best chocolate ever," she says. The type of brain-computer interface that Scheuermann and others have tested is not yet ready for use outside of a laboratory. After two years of working with the robotic arm, Scheuermann had to have her implants removed to avoid an infection.

Quoted in Kathryn Hulick, "One Day, Computers May Decode Your Dreams," Science News for Students, September 22, 2016. www.sciencenewsforstudents.org.

other sensations. "It feels great to have my hand back again," says Igor Spetic, who has helped test Tyler's technology.[57]

TMR is not the only way to give a person mind control over a robotic limb. The other option is to establish a brain-computer interface, which is a direct connection between the electrical signals in the brain and a computer. There are several ways to capture electrical signals from the brain, including using an EEG cap that registers brain waves. But brain waves are not precise enough to control a robotic limb. For such fine control, researchers currently have to perform brain surgery to implant electrodes in the parts of the brain that control movement. There the electrodes can detect the firing of specific brain cells. In the future, researchers hope to reach this level of precision in a mind-controlled device without having to perform brain surgery. "The long-term goal for all of this work is to have noninvasive—no extra surgeries, no extra implants—ways to control a dexterous robotic device," says Robert Armiger of Johns Hopkins University.[58]

dexterous

skilled at using the hands to perform tasks

Robotics technology can restore more than just missing limbs. By directly stimulating the optic nerve or the auditory nerve, bionic systems can restore sight to the blind and hearing to the deaf. The Argus II links a camera mounted in glasses to a computerized implant that passes information from the camera on to the brain. The system does not restore perfect vision. Users see contrast and edges in black and white, but that's enough to read large-print books or navigate unfamiliar spaces, and future updated versions could restore color vision. Cochlear implants for hearing work in a similar manner to transmit sounds directly to the brain.

cochlear

related to the inner part of the ear, which sends messages to the brain in response to sounds

All of these robotic implants make it clear that the future of medical robotics technology is not just about how robots will assist humans, but also about how humans will become increasingly robotic. As robots like Pepper learn to become more human in their mannerisms, humans will also become more robotic thanks to exoskeletons and implants. But most people do not seem to be too worried about how robotics technology will alter health care. In a 2017 survey by professional services group PricewaterhouseCoopers (PwC), the majority of respondents were willing to receive care from robots, especially if robotic care meant quicker access to services and more accurate diagnoses. People who were reluctant to engage with robots in health care said that they either did not trust robots or worried about the lack of a human touch. Tim Wilson of PwC says, "Whether we like it or not, AI and robotics are the future of healthcare. Access to quality, affordable healthcare, and good health for everyone are the ultimate goals."[59]

SOURCE NOTES

Introduction: Transforming Health Care

1. Quoted in Hannah Richardson, "Robots Could Help Solve Social Care Crisis, Say Academics," BBC News, January 30, 2017. www.bbc.com.
2. Quoted in Richardson, "Robots Could Help Solve Social Care Crisis, Say Academics."
3. Quoted in Mark Honigsbaum, "Meet the New Generation of Robotics. They're Almost Human . . . ," *Guardian* (Manchester, UK), September 15, 2003. www.theguardian.com.

Chapter 1: The First Robots

4. Quoted in Tekla S. Perry, "SRI's Pioneering Mobile Robot Shakey Honored as IEEE Milestone," IEEE Spectrum, February 17, 2017. http://spectrum.ieee.org.
5. Quoted in Sandra Blakeslee, "A Robot Arm Assists in 3 Brain Operations," *New York Times*, June 25, 1985. www.nytimes.com.
6. Quoted in Olga Lechky, "World's First Surgical Robot in B.C.," *Medical Post* (Toronto, Canada), November 12, 1985. www.brianday.ca.
7. Catherine Mohr, "Surgery's Past, Present, and Robotic Future," TED Talk, February 2009. www.ted.com.
8. Quoted in ASIMO, "ASIMO Inducted into Robot Hall of Fame," October 11, 2004. http://asimo.honda.com.

Chapter 2: Robotic Surgery

9. Quoted in Gina Kolata, "Results Unproven, Robotic Surgery Wins Converts," *New York Times*, February 13, 2010. www.nytimes.com.
10. Quoted in Commission for Technology and Innovation, "Laser-Cutting of Bones Replaces Sawing," July 2015. www.kti.admin.ch.

11. Quoted in Colorado CyberKnife, "Radiosurgery: What Is CyberKnife Robotic RadioSurgery?," YouTube, February 19, 2013. www.youtube.com.
12. Quoted in Tanya M. Anandan, "Robots and Healthcare Saving Lives Together," Robotic Industries Association, November 23, 2015. www.robotics.org.
13. Quoted in John Markoff, "New Research Center Aims to Develop Second Generation of Surgical Robots," *New York Times*, October 23, 2014. www.nytimes.com.
14. Quoted in Eliza Strickland, "Would You Trust a Robot Surgeon to Operate on You?," IEEE Spectrum, May 31, 2016. http://spectrum.ieee.org.
15. Quoted in Eliza Strickland, "Autonomous Robot Surgeon Bests Humans in World First," IEEE Spectrum, May 4, 2016. http://spectrum.ieee.org.
16. Quoted in Simon Parkin, "The Tiny Robots Revolutionizing Eye Surgery," *MIT Technology Review*, January 19, 2017. www.technologyreview.com.
17. Quoted in Helen Shen, "Meet the Soft, Cuddly Robots of the Future," *Nature*, February 3, 2016. www.nature.com.
18. Quoted in CBS News, "Flexible Robot Could Make Surgery, Recovery Easier," January 22, 2016. www.cbsnews.com.

Chapter 3: Helper Bots

19. Quoted in Matt Simon, "This Incredible Hospital Robot Is Saving Lives. Also, I Hate It," *Wired*, February 10, 2015. www.wired.com.
20. Thomas Boscher, "Boosting Hospital Operational Efficiency with Cleaning Robots," Sealed Air. https://sealedair.com.
21. Quoted in Claudia Buck, "Sutter's 'Germ-Zapping' Robot Latest Tool to Banish Deadly Hospital Infections," *Sacramento Bee*, March 13, 2017. www.sacbee.com.
22. Farhad Manjoo, "Will Robots Steal Your Job?," *Slate*, September 26, 2011. www.slate.com.
23. Quoted in Andrew Zaleski, "Behind Pharmacy Counter, Pill-Packing Robots Are on the Rise," CNBC, November 15, 2016. www.cnbc.com.
24. Quoted in Grant Gerke, "Automating the Preparation of Syringes and IV Bags," *AutomationWorld*, December 9, 2014. www.automationworld.com.

25. Quoted in Tekla S. Perry, "Profile: Veebot," IEEE Spectrum, July 26, 2013. http://spectrum.ieee.org.

Chapter 4: Diagnosis, Care, and Treatment

26. Quoted in Louise Chan, "Will Robots in Healthcare Make Doctors Obsolete?," *Tech Times*, February 9, 2016. www.techtimes.com.
27. Quoted in Jason Dorrier, "Telepresence Robots Invade Hospitals—'Doctors Can Be Anywhere, Anytime,'" Singularity-Hub, December 4, 2012. https://singularityhub.com.
28. Quoted in Sallie Jimenez, "Robots Being Designed to Assist Nurses, Not Replace Them," Nurse.com blog, December 29, 2016. www.nurse.com.
29. Quoted in UNC Lineberger, "Partnering with IBM and Watson to Accelerate DNA Analysis and Inform Personalized Treatment," May 5, 2015. https://unclineberger.org.
30. Quoted in Tomoko Otake, "IBM Big Data Used for Rapid Diagnosis of Rare Leukemia Case in Japan," *Japan Times*, August 11, 2016. www.japantimes.co.jp.
31. Quoted in Jonathan Cohn, "The Robot Will See You Now," *Atlantic*, March 2013. www.theatlantic.com.
32. Quoted in Siddhartha Mukherjee, "A.I. Versus M.D.," *New Yorker*, April 3, 2017. www.newyorker.com.
33. Quoted in Mukherjee, "A.I. Versus M.D."
34. Quoted in Renée Mickelburgh, "Meet Pearl—She's the Robo-Nurse Designed to Look After the Elderly," *Telegraph* (London), March 21, 2004. www.telegraph.co.uk.
35. Quoted in Reuters, "Robot Receptionist Gets Job at Belgian Hospital," YouTube, June 18, 2016. www.youtube.com.
36. Quoted in April Glaser, "Pepper, the Emotional Robot, Learns How to Feel Like an American," *Wired*, June 7, 2016. www.wired.com.
37. Quoted in Matthew J. Stock, "British Robot Helping Autistic Children with Their Social Skills," Reuters, March 31, 2017. www.reuters.com.
38. Quoted in Zora Bots, "Zora, the First Social Robot Already Widely Used in Healthcare," *Robotics Tomorrow*, April 12, 2016. www.roboticstomorrow.com.

39. Quoted in Anne Tergesen and Miho Inada, "It's Not a Stuffed Animal, It's a $6,000 Medical Device," *Wall Street Journal*, June 21, 2010. www.wsj.com.

40. Quoted in Mickelburgh, "Meet Pearl—She's the Robo-Nurse Designed to Look After the Elderly."

41. Louise Aronson, "The Future of Robot Caregivers," *New York Times*, July 19, 2014. www.nytimes.com.

42. Quoted in Caitlin Fairchild, "The Rise of the Health Care Robots," Nextgov, April 28, 2017. www.nextgov.com.

Chapter 5: From Therapy to Cyborgs

43. Quoted in ikinamo, "Home Care Robot, 'Yurina': DigInfo," YouTube, August 11, 2010. www.youtube.com.

44. Quoted in David Chandler, "Robot Wheelchair Finds Its Own Way," MIT News, September 19, 2008. http://news.mit.edu.

45. Quoted in Quil Lawrence, "A Reboot for Wheelchair That Can Stand Up and Climb Stairs," NPR, October 17, 2016. www.npr.org.

46. Quoted in Eamonn Tiernan, "ReWalk Exoskeleton Allows Paraplegic Paul Jenkins to Walk Again," *Sydney Morning Herald* (Australia), February 13, 2017. www.smh.com.au.

47. Quoted in Wyss Institute, "Soft Exosuits," https://wyss.harvard.edu.

48. David Boone, "Looking Ahead at Computer-Controlled Knees," *inMotion*, vol. 18, no. 7, November/December 2008. www.amputee-coalition.org.

49. Quoted in J.R. Wilson, "Prosthetics Meet Robotics," *Military & Aerospace Electronics*, October 8, 2013. www.militaryaerospace.com.

50. Quoted in Erico Guizzo, "Dean Kamen's 'Luke Arm' Prosthesis Receives FDA Approval," IEEE Spectrum, May 13, 2014. http://spectrum.ieee.org.

51. Quoted in Kerry McDermott, "Britain's First Bionic Boy: Patrick, 16, Overjoyed as He Gets Robotic Hand So Advanced It Can Be Controlled via Smartphone App," *Daily Mail* (London), April 23, 2013. www.dailymail.co.uk.

52. Quoted in Wilson, "Prosthetics Meet Robotics."

53. Quoted in Keith Oppenheim, "Jesse Sullivan Powers Robotic Arms with His Mind," CNN, March 23, 2006. www.cnn.com.

54. Quoted in Pam Belluck, "In New Procedure, Artificial Arm Listens to Brain," *New York Times*, February 10, 2009. www.nytimes.com.

55. Quoted in Celia Gorman and Jean Kumagai, "Prosthetic Hand Restores Amputee's Sense of Touch," IEEE Spectrum, May 17, 2016. http://spectrum.ieee.org.

56. Todd Kuiken, "A Prosthetic Arm That 'Feels,'" TED Talk, July 2011. www.ted.com.

57. Quoted in Gorman and Kumagai, "Prosthetic Hand Restores Amputee's Sense of Touch."

58. Quoted in Emma Cott, "Prosthetic Limbs, Controlled by Thought," *New York Times*, May 20, 2015. www.nytimes.com.

59. Quoted in PwC, "Consumers Ready to Embrace AI and Robots for Their Healthcare Needs," April 10, 2017. http://press.pwc.com.

Books

Malcom Gay, *The Brain Electric: The Dramatic High-Tech Race to Merge Minds and Machines*. New York: Farrar, Straus & Giroux, 2015.

John Markoff, *Machines of Loving Grace: The Quest for Common Ground Between Humans and Robots*. New York: HarperCollins, 2015.

Kenneth Partridge, ed., *Robotics*. New York: H.W. Wilson, 2010.

Clifford A. Pickover, *The Medical Book: From Witch Doctors to Robot Surgeons, 250 Milestones in the History of Medicine*. New York: Sterling, 2012.

Richard Spilsbury and Louise Spilsbury, *Robots in Medicine*. New York: Gareth Stevens, 2016.

Internet Sources

Tanya M. Anandan, "Robots and Healthcare Saving Lives Together," Robotic Industries Association, November 23, 2015. www.robotics.org/content-detail.cfm/Industrial-Robotics-Industry-Insights/Robots-and-Healthcare-Saving-Lives-Together/content_id/5819.

Len Calderone, "The Most Important Robots in Medicine," *Robotics Tomorrow*, June 20, 2017. www.roboticstomorrow.com/article/2017/06/the-most-important-robots-in-medicine/10201.

Jonathan Cohn, "The Robot Will See You Now," *Atlantic*, March 2013. www.theatlantic.com/magazine/archive/2013/03/the-robot-will-see-you-now/309216.

David von Drehle, "Meet Dr. Robot," *Time*, January 23, 2011. http://content.time.com/time/specials/packages/article/0,28804,2032747_2033111_2033133-2,00.html.

Siddhartha Mukherjee, "A.I. Versus M.D.," *New Yorker*, April 3, 2017. www.newyorker.com/magazine/2017/04/03/ai-versus-md.

Eliza Strickland, "Would You Trust a Robot Surgeon to Operate on You?," IEEE Spectrum, May 31, 2016. http://spectrum.ieee.org/robotics/medical-robots/would-you-trust-a-robot-surgeon-to-operate-on-you.

US National Library of Medicine, "Robotic Surgery," MedlinePlus. https://medlineplus.gov/ency/article/007339.htm.

Websites

IEEE Spectrum (http://spectrum.ieee.org/robotics/medical-robots). IEEE Spectrum is a magazine and website produced by IEEE, a professional organization for engineers and scientists. The website contains a section devoted to news about medical robots.

Mayo Clinic (www.mayoclinic.org/tests-procedures/robotic-surgery/basics/definition/prc-20013988). The Mayo Clinic presents helpful information on many medical procedures, including robotic surgery.

Medical Futurist (http://medicalfuturist.com). This blog presents news about the future of medicine, including robots, virtual reality, and more.

Robotic Industries Association (www.robotics.org). This website provides information to help companies and other organizations incorporate robotics and automation technology into their workflow.

INDEX

important events in history of, **6–7**

robot(s)
  earliest, 14–15
  flexible, 31–32
  jobs lost to, 19
  mobile, 33–35
  origin of term, 12
  See also specific types

RoNA (Robotic Nursing Assistant), 55–56

Roomba, 36

Rosen, Jacob, 29

Roy, Nicholas, 56

RP-7 robot, 42–43, **43,** 44

RP-VITA (Remote Presence Virtual + Independent Telemedicine Assistant), 44

R2-D2
  Star Wars character, 12, **13**
  See also Robotic Retinal Dissection Device

Ryan, Corey, 28

Sanchez, Justin, 61

Sandberg, Debbie, 37

Scheinman, Victor, 16

Scooba, 36

Shakey (robot), 15

Sharpless, Norman, 45

Smith, Jeffrey A., 21

social robots, 50–52

SoftBank Robotics, 49–50

Soft Robotics, 31

SpeciMinder, 35

Stanford Research Institute (SRI), 15

STAR (Smart Tissue Autonomous Robot), 29–30

surgical robots, 10
  for brain surgery, **16,** 16–17
  use in battlefields/disaster sites, 29

suture, 29
  definition of, 28

Takata, Yoshitaka, 56

targeted muscle reinnervation (TMR), 62
  definition of, 62

telepresence, 43–44, 45
  definition of, 11
  in surgery, 18

telepresence robots, 10, 42–44, 45

Theobald, Daniel, 39

Thorndyke, Brian, 27

Thrun, Sebastian, 47–48

Tojo, Arinobu, 46

TransEnterix, 24

Trauma Pod program, 29

TRINA (Tele-Robotic Intelligent Nursing Assistant), 44

PICTURE CREDITS

Kathryn Hulick is a freelance writer and former Peace Corps volunteer. After returning from two years teaching English in Kyrgyzstan, she started writing for children. Her books include *Careers in Robotics*, *Awesome Science: Dinosaurs*, and *Real-World STEM: Develop Fusion Energy*. She also contributes regularly to *Muse* magazine and the Science News for Students website. She enjoys hiking, painting, reading, and working in her garden. She lives in Massachusetts with her husband and son.